AMERICA'S GREAT PRIVATE GARDENS

Garden of Mrs. William P. Roth, San Mateo, California

AMERICA'S GREAT PRIVATE GARDENS

STANLEY SCHULER

The Macmillan Company, New York

COLLIER-MACMILLAN LTD., LONDON

Library of Congress Catalog Card Number: 67-12802

All photographs are by the author, unless otherwise noted.

First Printing

The Macmillan Company, New York
Collier-Macmillan Canada Ltd., Toronto, Ontario

Printed in the United States of America

Contents

Introduction

Of Beautiful Gardens, Climate, Geology, and Trends

As I write this foreword, I am on the island of Hawaii, the orchid-producing center of the United States and the only area where magnificent tree ferns compete with undistinguished lichens to become the first plants established on fresh lava flows. Yesterday I was on the north shore of the Island of Kauai in a tropical jungle garden which grows so lush that its owner has difficulty keeping it under control. Three days ago I was in Seattle, our northernmost major city, yet a city capable of growing more different kinds of plants than any other in the nation. Four days ago I was in Chicago, where a harsh climate has done much to discourage anything more than green gardens with large paved areas.

This is the country in which we live and in which we garden. In the past three months I have journeyed into almost every part of it except Alaska (where the climate is considerably less hospitable than in Chicago). I have been interested in two things: (1) Finding and photographing outstanding *private* (not open to the public) gardens and (2) learning how climate and geology affect them. The outcome of my research—but not my search, which is another matter—can hardly be surprising to anyone who is familiar with the physical character of our country. But I have made some interesting discoveries about gardens and gardening in general which merit airing:

Garden of Mr. and Mrs. Henry McIntyre, Hillsborough, California

*When you can sit on a concrete terrace under a broiling sun and feel cool—
that is a tribute to the magic of moving water*

1. To dispose of the key question first: Climate and geology *do* have an enormous effect on what you plant and how you landscape. True, there are many other things that influence these matters: the shape and contour of your lot; the size of your house and its location on the lot; the composition of your family; your personal preferences and prejudices; etc. But climate and geology (which to all intents and purposes means the soil) are of decisive importance. The surprising thing is that many people do not seem to know this.

Almost every landscape architect with whom I discussed the question reported that, when newcomers to the community ask for landscaping help, they usually think they can plant the same species they had in their previous gardens. In some cases, of course, this is possible. But when you move from New York to Phoenix, or Los Angeles to

Chicago, or Boston to Miami, there are very few plants that you can, in effect, take with you. The differences in climate and/or soil simply will not allow it. (Daylilies, incidentally, are the most notable exception I've encountered: they seem to thrive everywhere.)

In practical terms, what does this mean? Simply that if you should ever join the growing parade of people who are moving (or being moved) around the country, do not attempt to establish a garden in your new community until you have taken the time (and it does take time) to find out what will grow there *well*. A landscape architect can help you. So can a local nurseryman. One other source of information—visual if not always vocal—is the town's best cemetery. Landscape architectural students are often advised to visit a local cemetery if they are called on to develop grounds in a strange city.

Another trend is to plan and furnish the garden so it can be enjoyed more hours of the day

Garden of Mr. and Mrs. Clint Murchison, Sr., lighted by John Watson, Dallas

Garden of Mr. and Mrs. Arthur E. Benning. Photograph by John D. Eccles.

Climate and geology do *have an enormous effect on what you plant and how you landscape*

2. The worst threat to a *good* garden today is inability—perhaps combined with unwillingness—to use pruning shears. (Please note the accent on good gardens. Obviously, the worst threat to just any old garden is poor taste, lack of money, no sense of design—many things.)

Somehow most all of us seem to forget that plants grow quickly (assuming we have selected the kind that likes the local soil and climate). We put one in; step back and watch; and suddenly it is bigger than it should be; but we can't bring ourselves to do anything about it because it *is* so big and beautiful. Result: The garden is overgrown. It is crowded, featureless, oppressive, and after a while, because there isn't any sun, it is also colorless.

I can speak feelingly on this score because in my last house, after about fifteen years of faithful if exhausting attention to the clipping of a hemlock hedge, I gave up. And within the next five years the hedge grew so tall that it all but ruined my beautiful roses in its shadow.

If you have a good garden to start with, pruning is the key to its perpetuity. I do not know how you will get the pruning done—whether you will do it yourself or will hire someone to do it for you—but do it you must.

3. In ninety-nine cases out of one hundred, the owners of this country's outstanding gardens have gardeners. This must be, I fear, a discouraging thought to many people. It is, in truth, to me. But having been one of the fathers of the do-it-yourself movement, I must acknowledge facts.

A garden is demanding of attention—not just pruning, but watering, debugging, planting, mowing, etc. But many other things in life

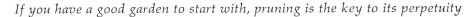

If you have a good garden to start with, pruning is the key to its perpetuity

Garden of Mrs. William P. Roth, San Mateo, California

are demanding, too. And that makes it well nigh impossible for any modern American affluent enough to start out with a good garden to keep it up by himself or, more likely, by herself.

But unfortunately, this fetches us right up against the No. 1 complaint of landscape architects and assiduous gardeners today: Good help is scarce. In fact, you might almost say there isn't any.

Here is one of the reasons why gardens become overgrown.

Here also is the reason why so much emphasis is placed on easy-maintenance gardens. There just is no escaping the fact that there is a strong trend to these, and I, for one, am rather sorry to see it. Figur-

Each garden is very much the product—the reflection—of its owner

Garden of Mr. and Mrs. Frederick W. Beinecke

ing out ways to keep grass from spreading into flower beds, to eliminate edging, to move power mowers easily from one area to another—maintenance-reducing steps of this nature are one thing. But when the effort to save work leads to the elimination from the garden of annuals and perennials and other somewhat demanding flowering plants, that is going too far. Green gardens can be very lovely (as those in this book prove); but as a rule, gardens with well-chosen, well-placed color have the edge.

4. At the very time when more and more new varieties of plants are being developed or discovered, the selection available to gardeners is growing more limited. A paradox? Yes, but understandable.

There are fads in plants as in many other things. (The current fad is azaleas—bluish-red azaleas which custom says must always be planted alongside the brightest orange-red azaleas one can buy.) How these start I do not know. Sometimes the public is responsible; sometimes the growers. But the long-range effect is to persuade the average nurseryman and retail garden center operator to raise and sell only the relatively few species and varieties that John Q. Public wants. And since JQP does not know that there are many other and perhaps better kinds of plants, he does not think to demand them.

Admittedly, experienced gardeners and landscape architects usually are able to ferret out the choicer items. But this often takes a lot of doing. Perhaps in self-defense and out of kindness to ordinary gardeners, they should try to start a few fads of their own. Or more should follow the splendid examples of Mrs. Pendleton Miller and Mr. Epstein, both of whom have spent years seeking out and testing new and better plants.

5. Another trend—a much happier one—is to plan and furnish the garden so it can be enjoyed more hours of the day and more days of the year. This is most clearly evidenced by the number of gardens that have outdoor lighting for purely decorative purposes. I failed to keep count, but I guess that fully half of the gardens I show here have extensive lighting systems.

Covered terraces or porches, somewhat surprisingly, are not so common as you might think—at least among the owners of outstanding gardens. But the gazebo is returning (or has never left us)—and many of them are large enough for use in wet weather (yes, a garden can be charming in the rain or fog).

6. The sound and sight of moving water—an ancient idea—is a feature of an increasing number of gardens and a most delightful one. From the tiny, tiny water spout in Mr. Lannan's garden to the whirling fountain in Mrs. Herter's, I liked them all. I saw nothing, however, to equal the magnificent combination of fountains and steps and rippling channels that Mr. and Mrs. McIntyre have. When you can sit on a concrete terrace surrounded by concrete walls on a clear spring day under a broiling noonday sun and *feel cool*—that is a tribute to the magic of moving water and most especially to the McIntyres' inspiration.

7. To get back to the differences between gardens—I was, as I roamed the country, frankly amazed that these can be so great. It occurred to me somewhere along the line that we have been led to believe by the FBI and the like that nothing is so individualistic, so distinctive as a set of fingerprints. What nonsense! A garden—yours, mine, anyone's—is a hundred times more so.

Consider the gardens here. No two are alike (and I did not plan it that way). Each is a product of the climate and geology of its locale. Yes, and each is very much the product—the reflection—of its owner and, to considerable extent, its landscape architect.

This perhaps is the real key to what makes a garden outstanding. It is the expression of the individual who creates it and who lives with it. It is Mr. Edwin Beinecke's fantastic collection of rhododendrons and azaleas or Mrs. Hortense Miller's ever-widening collection of many genera and species. It is Mrs. Wichman's dense jungle garden or Mr. and Mrs. McCullough's wide-open, hilltop garden. It is the whimsical little garden of Mrs. Chandler or the big, formal garden of the late Mr. and Mrs. Backus. It is the flower-packed garden of Mrs. Banks or the green garden of Mr. and Mrs. Schamberg. It is the large, leisurely, nostalgic garden of Mr. and Mrs. Webster or the small, modern, fairyland garden of Mr. and Mrs. Murchison.

All these gardens are different; but all have one all-important thing in common: They do not hesitate to say—though always quietly and with exquisite taste—"I am my owner"—an individual, fresh and exciting.

*From Mrs. Kennedy's house the lawn flows down, around a rose garden,
into a stepped-down area that is green in summer but water-filled in winter*

Garden of

Mrs. Audrey K. Kennedy

Brookline, Massachusetts

M RS. KENNEDY is the owner of two exceptional gardens. They are quite different—not simply because of differences in climate and topography but also because landscape architect Stanley Underhill felt his client would appreciate a change of pace. Consequently, one of his objectives in developing this garden in Brookline was to avoid using too many of the same flowering broadleaf evergreens he expected to use in Mrs. Kennedy's garden in Southern Pines.

Mr. Underhill's other aims were (1) to preserve as many of the great trees as he possibly could (this was an order from Mrs. Kennedy) and (2) to make sparing use of perennials, annuals, and other small flowering plants that require considerable attention.

The tree-saving objective was the hardest, but was attained: only one tree was removed. There were other problems, however. For one thing, a large amount of fill had to be brought in to counteract the steepness of the slope on which the house and terrace were built. At the last minute, a turnaround in front of the garage had to be relocated. And an enormous dry well had to be built to soak up some of the rain and snow water that became trapped in a pocket at the foot of the lawn every winter.

Except for the fact that the lawn pocket still floods, you are not aware of any of these construction problems today. On the contrary, the garden looks as if it had come about almost naturally. It is informal and serene—a garden for sauntering.

It has several standout features: The grand trees. A couple of big, rough glacial boulders of a type known locally as puddingstone. Half a dozen or so beguiling little statues. And shrubbery borders to make you envious forever.

The fact that the last are so thick, varied, and attractive speaks well for Mr. Underhill's ability to find plenty of worthy genera different

Mountain laurel and other handsome shrubs crowd against the steps from the paved terrace to the rear lawn. Shrubs are garden's main color element.

Small, flat hilltop that protects the house (unseen to left) *from sweeping driveway* (right and rear) *is a cool, inviting oasis under the ancient trees*

from those in Mrs. Kennedy's southern garden. It is also an indication that Boston does not have such a fiendish climate and geology as non-New Englanders suppose.

Boston (and Brookline) is in the warmer section of Zone 6; but most of the suburbs to the west are in the colder section of the zone, and you do not have to go far beyond them to hit Zone 5. Over the years the temperature in the city proper has ranged from a rock-bottom minus 18 to a high of 104. Precipitation averages almost 43 inches a year.

The soil is spotty but Mr. Underhill considers it to be generally good. The most common geological problem in the area is the presence of innumerable swamps and hard-to-drain low spots left by the great glaciers. The usual practice—now bitterly opposed by conservationists—is to fill these in. But they have their own rather attractive flora; and if not spring fed, they dry up in warm weather and can support grass and many perennials.

Woody plants in Mrs. Kennedy's garden include the following:

Beech, European
Birch, gray
Cotinus coggygria
Cotoneaster, adpressa, decora, and *divaricata*
Dogwood, kousa
Elaeagnus angustifolia
Enkianthus campanulatus
Euonymus alatus
Hemlock, Canadian and Sargent's weeping
Holly (*Ilex convexa* and *glabra*)
Honeysuckle, yellow bush
Juniper (various kinds)
Leucothoe catesbaei
Lilac (*Syringa japonica* and hybrids)
Mountain laurel
Oak, pin and red
Pieris japonica
Pine, white
Potentilla (various kinds)
Rhododendron hybrids
Rose of Sharon
Spirea Anthony Waterer
Viburnum dentatum
Vitex macrophylla
Willow, purple osier
Yew (various kinds)

From the tree-shaded hilltop (page 13) you look down over the shrub-packed rock garden to terrace off the living room. Rear lawn is below wall at right.

Curved redwood screen at end of the Jeffries' garden serves as a comfortable backdrop for plants and also conceals toolshed and parking space behind

Garden of

Mr. and Mrs. Benjamin E. Jeffries

Boston, Massachusetts

THERE IS always a danger that small city gardens will look boxy and confining. This one, measuring only 18 by 40 feet, is neither.

Though the garden is a rectangle, landscape architect Stanley Underhill avoided a boxy look by repeated use of curved lines. The simple but graceful redwood screen that hides a small tool shed and parking space at the rear of the garden makes an arc that matches the big bowed windows at the back of the house. The border of evergreens at the base of the screen is curved in another way; and a raised herb border along the left wall is also curved. And the paved area between the two borders—made of small granite blocks—not only is curved along the edges but is also laid out in an intricate pattern of small overlapping fans.

In addition to introducing pleasing lines and texture to the garden, the block paving serves a second purpose: It separates the smooth brick paving at the ends of the garden and thus makes the garden look shorter and wider than it actually is. Conceivably, it might also act as a subtle visual barrier that keeps the Jeffries' children from scattering toys and sand outside the bricked area that constitutes their play yard.

The fence on the sides of the garden is another fine textural element. It is made of boards and large half rounds slightly separated.

Outside of the herbs, planting in the garden is restricted mainly to a few azaleas, rhododendrons, enkianthus, bulbs, and *Vinca minor*. After these bloom in the spring, the garden is essentially green, gray, brown, and brick red.

One reason for the curved lines and change in paving is to make the garden appear as attractive from the upper floors of house as from the ground level

Raised bed curving in toward center of garden helps to make the garden look shorter, provides change in elevation, and protects herbs from the children

Although summers are short and winters harsh in the Berkshires, they do not stop Mrs. Beinecke from raising annuals and perennials in incredible array

Garden of

Mr. and Mrs. Frederick W. Beinecke

Great Barrington, Massachusetts

WHEN I first approached Mr. and Mrs. Beinecke about photographing their garden, Mrs. Beinecke wrote me: "This is a very modest garden. We have many beautiful flowers, yes, but the severe Berkshire winters and the extremely short growing season (we have had frost as late as June 3 and as early as the last week in August) limit us very much and necessitate the production of innumerable annuals to fill in."

All I can say to this is: If a rugged climate is to blame for this colorful garden, would that more gardeners had to cope with an equally rugged climate!

Actually, there *is* something about the Berkshires' climate and rocky soil that produces marvelous flowers—and particularly marvelous delphinium, clematis, and tuberous begonias. But it is obvious that Mrs. Beinecke deserves most of the credit for the rainbow that is her garden. She grows almost every flower in the popular catalogues. She grows scads of them: her cutting garden alone is well over half an acre. And she grows them well.

Although the cutting garden's masses of color are what you are likely to remember longest after visiting the Beineckes' place, they do not overshadow the rest of the garden when you are there. I cannot explain why this is, because the entire garden is extremely informal and unpretentious—designed simply for easygoing summer living.

Paralleling the road is a split-rail fence with a single shell-pink, red, or yellow climbing rose between each pair of posts. The big, casual front lawn is partially shaded by old trees that appear to have been placed by the Beineckes' predecessors with as little reason as the inevitable New England boulders that stick up through the grass. Two

Sunken garden behind house (unseen to left) *is brilliant with pink roses and perennials and on clear days commands a view of the mountains to the north*

Covered terrace at end of Mr. Beinecke's workshop centers on path bordered by cutting garden (behind fence) *and rose and delphinium garden* (right)

pleasant little terraces made bright with potted tuberous begonias and geraniums are set into corners of the rambling white house. Here and there under clumps of trees or shrubs Mrs. Beinecke has set out other pots of flowers.

The least casual area is a small, rectangular garden with low rock walls tucked into the side of the hill behind the house. It is planted with pink roses and assorted perennials; and on the outside of the

This little terrace outside dining room is one of two tucked into corners of the old house. Tuberous begonias grow here as well as on Monterey Peninsula.

More tuberous begonias and other shade-loving plants flourish in the lath-house outside Mr. Beinecke's workshop. "It's been a joy," Mrs. Beinecke says.

downhill wall are more tall perennials, wonderful lilies, and two large Russian olives. Standing at the south end of the garden, you look north across it to distant mountains. From the north end, you look south through an opening in a row of conifers to the cutting garden. Both views are typical of what you hope to find in New England—but only sometimes do.

Handsome approach to Edwin Beinecke house includes only a few of the rhododendrons and azaleas for which the surrounding big garden is famed

Garden of

Mr. and Mrs. Edwin J. Beinecke

Greenwich, Connecticut

MR. AND MRS. BEINECKES' COLLECTION of rhododendrons and azaleas is one of the country's greatest. Their narcissus collection is immense. Tall trees, great rocks, and rugged hills give their land a quiet splendor.

When it is at its height in the spring, their garden takes your breath away. In less colorful seasons, it is—simply—magnificent.

In 1945, when the Beineckes (he is the brother of Frederick W. of Great Barrington) built their Greenwich home, they asked the Long Island landscape architectural firm of Innocenti & Webel to develop the land immediately around it. Taking his cue from the big Georgian residence, Mr. Webel came up with a plan for a large, parklike area including a grand approach to the house, a gracious terrace, a shrub-bordered lawn, a small swimming pool and a rock garden that is almost straight up and down. This area is little changed today. Despite weathering and the growth made by the trees and shrubs, it remains quite formal and very handsome. But it is only an incidental reason for the superlatives that mere mention of the Beinecke garden evokes from people who have seen it.

The great show is the twenty-five acre woodland garden that Mr. Beinecke and his superintendent, Alfred Woodger, have developed over the past two decades.

*Two huge **Taxus** espaliers blanket the wall supporting the rear terrace. The first was planted in 1946 by Superintendent Woodger and was later divided.*

Shortly before the dogwoods bloom, the hilly land turns gay with enormous drifts of yellow and white narcissus. There are more than two hundred kinds.

In late April and early May it is carpeted with narcissus—250,000 bulbs of more than two hundred varieties producing well over one million blooms. Then come the dogwoods—a sea of white. And then, usually about May 28, the rhododendrons and azaleas reach their height.

There is no describing this scene. Mr. Woodger estimates that he has put in more than ten thousand plants—not seedlings but full-size specimens. They include almost every variety that will survive a southern Connecticut winter plus a good many that could not if they were planted in a less favorable situation. (Up to a few years ago, Mr. Beinecke annually shipped in two truckloads of Oregon rhododendrons; but he gave up the practice when many of the plants proved to be of doubtful hardiness.) The colors of the massed plants range from the usual whites, pinks, reds, and purples to the less familiar yellows, oranges, and blues.

That plants of such size and brilliance would be spectacular anywhere is, of course, obvious. But they gain impact from the natural backdrop against which they are placed here.

Greenwich is a town of wispy soil and massive rocks. To provide enough depth of soil for his rhododendrons, Mr. Beinecke has the thin layers of humusy soil that have built up over many years on the rock outcroppings stripped off and spread out in the valleys at the base of the rocks. Then he has the rocks washed down with high-pressure hoses to give a clean, gray, sometimes smooth, sometimes fissured background for the flowers. You have never seen finer.

*Massive granite outcroppings and towering trees form the backdrop for one
of world's greatest, still growing displays of rhododendrons and azaleas*

Wild fowl are the No. 1 feature of the Hesses' open-space garden; the willow-overhung pond is its pivot point. Wire fence keeps the birds off fine lawn.

Garden of

Mr. and Mrs. Thomas B. Hess

Greenwich, Connecticut

THERE ARE some people who feel that a garden to be a garden must be filled with plants and flower beds. James Fanning is a landscape architect who believes that well-planned, uncluttered open space can be beautiful too.

In the case of this garden, Mr. Fanning had the best possible excuse for holding to this belief. Mr. and Mrs. Hess wanted, before anything else, a clear view of the wild ducks, geese, and swans that populate the large pond which bisects their property. They have it. But in giving it to them, Mr. Fanning actually put in more plants than he took out.

"Most views are improved if they are framed," he says. "The frame helps to keep your attention focused. And if it is close to you, it helps you to judge the scale of whatever the view features.

"On Mr. and Mrs. Hess's place, the view of the pond downhill behind the house was framed on the right—as you sat on the terrace or inside the house—by a funny old Victorian root cellar, a stone wall, and a broken row of trees. But there was nothing really on the left to keep the eye from wandering. Furthermore, if you looked far enough to the left, you bumped into a service road and the vegetable garden. So we put in a large planting of lilacs to frame the view on that side."

Other plants of varying size have also been set out. For instance, a copper beech at the left end of the house extends the lines of the house, blocks the public view of the terrace and lawn area that the family usually occupies, and will eventually shade the sunporch. The rows of pink horse chestnuts—one of Mrs. Hess's favorite trees—frame the corner of the meadow used as a play field. More lilacs and a small arbor of pleached cherry trees pretty up the swimming pool area and adjacent party house (both of which are visible across the duck pond from the terrace of the main house). A beautiful cutting garden with an unusual path pattern flourishes in what had been an old riding ring.

Admittedly, no one belonging to the heavy-planting school of thought would feel that these few efforts have turned Mr. and Mrs.

The cutting garden has a few unusually large beds laid out in long curves and so planted that at any time there is at least one bed solid with bloom

Old and young flowering fruit trees team with recently planted lilacs and horse chestnuts (not shown) to bring springtime color to the big lawn areas

Hess's place into what *he* would call a garden. And I must agree that the land still seems very open and unadorned (after all, the new trees and shrubs are far from their ultimate size). But a garden it is—with simplicity, color, interest, and sweep (a very nice combination of qualities).

*Carefully planted rock outcroppings stud the irregular stretches of lawn
which Mr. Epstein has woven in among the trees and bordered with color*

Garden of

Mr. and Mrs. Harold Epstein

Larchmont, New York

Mr. EPSTEIN is one of the country's great plantsmen. Unlike other fine plantsmen, he is also an excellent gardener and landscape designer.

His garden is a little over one acre in extent. He and his wife purchased the place thirty years ago; the only things that still remain are the rock ledges and the big trees. Mr. Epstein has remodeled everything else not once but several times (he believes that gardens need to be "reupholstered" regularly if they are not to get out of hand). He filled in a swampy area. He moved many of the rocks. And he planted and planted and planted some more.

On any clear day the garden is sun-dappled and cool. But you cannot just relax and enjoy one spot. There are too many delights beckoning to you: A steep rock garden with several tiny, still pools (actually, the whole place is often called a rock garden; but this small area just below the house is definitely one). Long, irregular stretches of lawn studded with gray rock outcroppings and almost always with color masses at the ends. A cliff banked with rhododendrons. Shaded glens. Little walks winding through trees and flowering shrubs.

Wherever you go, however, the standout attractions are the plants. Mr. Epstein specializes in raising rare plants, many of them minia-

This is Mr. Epstein's jewel garden—so-called because it is filled with almost two hundred of the horticultural gems that he seeks from around the world

Garden between house and driveway was developed out of rocks moved from elsewhere on property. Mr. Epstein rebuilds and replants constantly.

GARDEN OF MR. AND MRS. HAROLD EPSTEIN   39

tures. And although his taste is catholic, the fact that the soil in his garden is acid explains the concentration on the Ericaceae. At one time, some years ago, he kept a card file describing every plant in the garden; but when this task began to take more time than actual gardening, he gave it up. Today he does not know exactly what is in the garden but estimates there are well over two thousand species and varieties. In just one five-by-twenty-five-foot bed, which he calls his jewel garden because it is planted to nothing but especially choice miniatures, there are over one hundred and eighty different plants.

Why Mr. Epstein cultivates such a wide range of plants is explained in two paragraphs he once wrote:

"The keen horticulturist must surely be aware of the diminishing sources and supply of choice and distinctive plants, particularly those slow or difficult to propagate. Postwar economics in this country, with constantly increasing costs, are responsible. The many prewar nurseries that had excellent assortments of plant species have gradually gone out of business or have resorted to cultivating conventional plants of easy and fast growth. Such plants carry these same characters into the garden, consequently requiring special care and control to restrain their growth.

"The gradual decrease in the scope and size of many gardens has taught the serious gardener to be more selective in choosing his plants. But the availability of true horticultural jewels has become extremely limited, and the search for them has become a time-consuming and challenging task."

For Mr. Epstein the task is indeed consuming. He travels the world over searching for new, forgotten, and overlooked plants and superior clones. His correspondence with other horticulturists, both professional and amateur, is voluminous. And when he isn't traveling or writing letters, he is in his garden testing and evaluating plants, both new and old, to see how well they perform. He also does considerable propagating and distributing of his rarities.

"I am a bloodhound about plants," he told me. "But I am not interested in plants just because they are rare. They must first of all be interesting, distinctive, dependable—worth growing in the East."

The success of Mr. Epstein's efforts—which are of value to all gardeners, not just to himself—is clear when you visit his garden.

*One of the delights of the garden is suddenly to come upon rare azaleas and
other plants tucked into places that less dedicated gardeners would ignore*

This is a small part of the Websters' formal garden, once a Victory garden.
Beyond fence, grounds stretch toward driveway and house (unseen to right).

Garden of

Mr. and Mrs. Charles D. Webster

Islip, New York

Mr. WEBSTER has called his garden a "horticultural zoo." The phrase is apt but unfair to the Websters. Their garden is far more than a large collection of plants (and an almost equally large collection of birds ranging from peacocks down). It is a spacious, comfortable, beautifully tailored thing with much of the feeling of your grandfather's old place (it happens to have been Mrs. Websters' grandfather's place). It is sitting under an apple tree and letting the breezes wash over you on a warm, lazy day. It is idling through the cottage garden with its white picket fence and neat paths. It is peering down the long lawn and through the tunnel of trees in hopes of spying a white sail ghosting through the mists of Great South Bay.

What I am trying to say is that Mr. and Mrs. Webster's garden is full of nostalgia. And not surprisingly, because the house and land date their current-day development to somewhere around 1870.

Mr. and Mrs. Webster made the place their year-round residence in 1946. They have been expanding the garden ever since. Among other things, they remade the picketed garden, which an early tenant had started as a Victory garden, into a formal flower garden with an octagonal lathhouse; built a terrace and a couple of well-filled greenhouses; planted a holly border, a viburnum border, and an apple

Formal garden revolves around octagonal lathhouse. It is divided into formal beds, paths, knot garden, etc. Potting houses and toolhouse adjoin (left).

orchard; dug a duck pond which they hedged around with various conifers and berried shrubs; and set up a big, wire-enclosed fruit cage to ensure that they and not the birds might enjoy their berry-growing efforts.

This recitation gives some idea of the Websters' wide-ranging gardening interests. But one interest is paramount: They like to raise plants—all kinds of plants that will do well in their particular part of Long Island.

Several years ago Mr. Webster described the climate and geology he and his wife have to contend with in the following manner:

"Twyford is on the south shore of Long Island in an area once composed of brackish saltwater creeks and marshland interspersed with stands of native shrubs and trees. The soil is shallow, sandy, and acid, suitable for plants in the Ericaceous range. A water table, subject to tidal influences, rises at times within 30 inches of the upper soil level. By the addition of mulches of manure and compost and by a careful feeding program, cultivated plants in wider ranges have been adapted to the garden. The temperature hardiness range lies in the upper half of Zone 7, quite temperate but susceptible to rapid variation in December, January, and February. There is generally no deep frost. High northwest winds and lack of winter snow cover often prove hazardous to woody plants, trees, and shrubs."

Plants grown by the Websters are the following (I have changed some of the botanical names to common names):

Albizzia julibrissin rosea
Alchemilla vulgaris
Ampelopsis brevipedunculata
Aristolochia durior
Aronia arbutifolia
Azalea arborescens, Glenn Dales, and other hybrids
Barberry (*Berberis juliana, mentorensis, and veruculosa*)
Beach plum
Benzoin aestivale
Birch, white and gray
Blueberry, high-bush
Box (*Buxus arborescens*, Korean, *microphylla* (Kingsville), *sempervirens*, and Vardar Valley)
Caryopteris Blue Mist
Cherry laurel
Chestnut, Bartlett's resistant strain
Chionanthus virginica

Clethra alnifolia, rosea, and *fargesii*
Corylopsis sinensis
Cotoneaster dammeri, glaucophylla, horizontalis, and *microphylla*
Crabapple (*Malus floribunda*)
Davidia involucrata
Dogwood (*Cornus florida, alternifolia, kousa, mas, nuttalli, sanguinea,* and
　　stolonifera)
Elaeagnus angustifolia, longipes, pungens, and *umbellata*
Enkianthus campanulatus and *cernuus rubus*
Erica alba and *darleyensis*
Euonymus alatus compactus
Fir (*Abies concolor* and *nordmanniana*)
Gordonia alatamaha and *lasianthus*
Hackberry
Halesia carolina
Hawthorn (*Crataegus carrierei*)
Heather (*Calluna rigida* and Beale's)
Hemlock, Carolina
Hinoki cypress

*Along one side of formal garden a border laid out in diamond shape bespeaks
the quiet elegance and nostalgic air of the entire well-tailored property*

Holly (*aqui-pernyii, burfordii, centrochinensis, cornuta, crenata, glabra, ilex aquifolium, latifolia, opaca, pedunculosa, rotundifolia, rugosa,* and *virticillata*)

Honeylocust

Iberis

Ivy, Mandas crested

Jasminum nudiflorum

Kerria japonica

Leiophyllum buxifolium

Loropetalum chinense

Magnolia acuminata, cordata, glauca, and *stellata*

Mahonia aquifolium

Maple, silver and sugar; also *Acer griseum*

Metasequoia glyptostroboides

Mountain laurel

Oak, burr, pyramidal, white, and willow

Osmanthus burkwoodii, ilicifolia, and *rotundifolia*

Oxydendrum arboreum

Photinia villosa

Pieris floribunda and *japonica*

Pine, Austrian, foxtail, Japanese black, Swiss stone, and white

Poncirus trifoliata

Pontentilla vilmoriniana and others

Pseudolarix amabilis

Redbud

Rhodondendron carolinianum, keiskei, myrtifolia, racemosum, vaseyi, wilsonii, and hybrids

Sarcocca hookeriana and *hookeriana humilis*

Skimmia laureola

Spruce, Norway; also *Picea obovata* and *orientalis*

Stewartia camelliofolia, koreana, monadelpha, ovata, serrata, and *sinensis*

Styrax japonica and *obassia*

Symplocos paniculata

Tupelo

Umbrella pine

Viburnum bracteatum, burejaeticum, burkwoodii, carlcephalum, carlesii, cassinoides, chenaultii, cotinifolium, dentatum, dilatatum, erosum, foetans, fragrans, glomeratum, hanceanum, hirtulum, ichangense, japonicum, juddii, lantana, macrocephalum, nudum, opulus, plicatum, prunifolium, rhytidophylloides, sargentii, sieboldii, theiferum, tomentosum, trilobum, utile, wrightii

Vitex agnus-castus and *negundo*

Witch hazel

Willow (*Salix tortuosa*)

Yellow-wood

Yew (*Taxus hatfieldii* and *nana*)

Zelkova

Swimming pool is most modern feature of the Pecks' garden, which dates to 1813. It is surrounded by strips of grass and pink, white, and yellow bloom.

Garden of

Mr. and Mrs. Frederick W. G. Peck

Chestnut Hill, Philadelphia, Pennsylvania

THIS GARDEN has gone through four distinct stages.

When it was established about 1813 by a French count who had his heart set on raising silkworms, it was a rather formal affair with boxwood-lined paths, a high stone wall, and an *allée* of mulberry trees. Some ninety years later it was redesigned by Olmsted Brothers, noted Boston landscape architects, and developed by its owners (with the help of fifteen full-time gardeners) into one of Philadelphia's most distinguished formal gardens. After it was purchased by the Pecks in 1951, Mr. Peck, who is a landscape architect, removed some of the boxwood in deference to modern living requirements, replanted the borders, and added the terrace and teahouse. Then in March of 1958 came an unusually severe snowstorm. "All that night we could hear the branches of the old boxwood snapping," Mr. Peck recalls. "When the snow melted days later, many of the plants were hopelessly damaged and had to be removed."

And so the garden was redesigned again. Looking at it today, you are rather thankful for the snowstorm. It turned a fine garden into a better one—one that retains some of its old formality but very definitely belongs to the 1960s; one in which masses of color replace masses of blackish green.

A main reason why the Pecks' garden still rates among Philadelphia's very finest is that it has so many points of interest: The shaded, two-level terrace. The teahouse with a translucent back that glows with light in the afternoon sun. A circular pool with a short spout of water splashing on the tummy of a seal. An *allée* of styrax trees with a fine underplanting of rhododendrons, azaleas, and smaller flowers. A swimming pool and behind it an inviting guesthouse. A formal garden with a pair of topiary yews. Several stretches of well-kept lawn. And here and there clumps of billowy boxwood, no longer oppressive, now simply protective.

No matter where you stand in the garden, one or more of these varied elements occupies the center of the stage. In consequence, no

Allée of styrax trees bisects area between guesthouse (right) *and main house. Shrubs and flowers under trees are one of the garden's strong color elements.*

Teahouse in corner of garden glows in the late afternoon sun. Although it calls attention to itself, it shuts off the view of a large house next door.

part of the garden is dull. As you move around in it, you constantly encounter something new, interesting, and pleasant.

The second reason for the garden's success lies in the beauty and variety of the planting. Philadelphia has the best climate of any eastern city for growing things. Its worst fault, Mr. Peck believes, is the wind. This is rarely severe, but in winter it can damage broadleaf evergreens. But here the Pecks are in luck, because the old stone wall and the boxwood afford such protection that the garden even boasts fine specimens of both *Magnolia grandiflora* and crepe myrtle.

Other plants that do well in the garden—not counting the host of perennials and bulbs that Mr. Peck likes to work over—are the following:

Ampelopsis heterophylla
Azalea coccinea, indica, schlippenbachii, and hybrids
Barberry, warty
Beech, European
Bignonia Mme. Galen
Cedar, blue Atlas
Cherry, flowering—black, kwanzan, pyramidal, and white
Clematis henryi, jackmanii, lanuginosa, lawsoniana, montana, and hybrids
Clethra alnifolia
Crabapple, crimson, Siberian, and weeping
Cytisus praecox
Daphne cneorum
Dogwood, Florida and kousa
Elaeagnus pungens
Enkianthus campanulatus
Euonymus radicans
Golden-chain tree
Hedera helix
Hemlock, Canadian
Holly (*Ilex aquifolium, burfordii, ciliospinosa, glabra, helleri,* and *opaca*)
Jasminum nudiflorum
Leucothoe catesbaei trivar
Maackia amurensis
Magnolia acuminata, cordata, and *glauca-virginiana*
Mahonia aquifolium
Mockorange named varieties
Mountain laurel
Neillia sinensis
Oak, black
Osmanthus fortunei
Oxydendrum arboreum
Pieris japonica
Pine, mugo and white
Potentilla Katherine Dykes
Pyracantha lalandii
Quince, dwarf flowering
Rhododendron hybrids
Rosa hugonis
St. Johnswort
Skimmia japonica
Stewartia pseudo-camellia
Styrax japonica
Tulip tree
Wisteria floribunda longissima
Yellow-wood
Yew (*Taxus baccata and capitata*)

Once dominated by somnolent mounds of dark boxwood, the Pecks' ancient garden is today alive with exciting color and a variety of interesting forms

The sinuous flower bed that cuts across the Clarks' wide, slightly sloping rear lawn gives it at once a feeling of useful immediacy and great depth

Garden of

Mr. and Mrs. George R. Clark

Flourtown, Pennsylvania

THE SOIL in eastern Pennsylvania varies considerably. In Lancaster County it is fabulously fertile. In Philadelphia it is best characterized as indifferent. There is clay in some spots; rock in others. The topsoil is thin, needs humus and sometimes sand, and a good deal of fertilizer.

In Mr. and Mrs. Clark's garden, there is one additional soil problem—a most unusual problem to be sure; but it points up the fact once again that gardens and gardening differ widely. A mile or so away is a lime kiln; and when the wind is blowing from the west, it deposits layers of lime dust on the garden. The result is that the pH of the soil is high enough to make it far more difficult to grow acid-loving broadleaf evergreens here than elsewhere in the Philadelphia area.

This, however, has not prevented the Clarks and their landscape architect, Frederick W. G. Peck, from creating a bright, thriving, and charming garden.

One of Mr. Peck's basic beliefs is that, in landscaping, design is everything. "You don't need unusual plants and other features to have a great garden," he says. "Of course you need good plants. But the main question is to put things together so they look as if they belong together."

Colorful border makes possible a definite drop in lawn elevation while con-cealing the fact that there is a drop. The flowers change with the seasons.

In the Clark garden, things go together perfectly. All the individual elements are in harmony between themselves and with the land. And almost from the moment you first enter it, you have the very strong feeling that the entire garden is in unusually close harmony with the house, the original part of which was built in 1764. Not that it is the kind of garden the first owner of the house would have had. Indeed, the only parts suggestive of the Colonial period are the boxwood-lined front walk and the Chippendale fence separating the main lawn area from the diamond-shaped combination cutting and vegetable garden. But the garden somehow gives the impression that it was designed especially to show off the house. And the house, in turn, looks as if it were made to show off the garden.

Both Mr. and Mrs. Clark are devoted gardeners. Their borders, whether filled with shrubs or with flowers or with both, abound in color and texture. Those that are planted mainly to peonies and/or lilies make the most stunning show. But there are various small planting areas with enormous appeal. I stumbled on one of these tucked into a shaded, out-of-the-way spot that most gardeners would not have bothered with. It was quilted with dicentra and heuchera and other little flowers. The blossoms were tiny; the colors, quiet. But the total effect was captivating—all because the Clarks put as much thought and work into developing the small areas as the large.

Chippendale fence in keeping with the lines of the fine old house separates cutting and vegetable garden (unseen to left) *from the sweeping lawn area*

Mrs. Herter's garden was paved with brick when her efforts to grow grass proved ineffective. The garden lies one floor below the main floor of house.

Garden of

Mrs. Christian A. Herter

Washington, D.C.

PLANTS GENERALLY LIKE Washington's climate better than people do. The exception is grass. "This is the worst place in the country for grass," landscape architect Perry H. Wheeler claims. "It's too far south for northern grasses; too far north for southern grasses. Consequently, they either burn out or are killed by fungus."

The problems of maintaining a lawn in back of their Georgetown home are what prompted Mrs. Herter and her late husband to ask Mr. Wheeler to redo this small, walled, partially shaded area several years ago. The garden is now as practical as it is charming.

The old lawn area is paved with bricks laid tight together on a bed of sand. In the center is a small square pool set at a 45-degree angle to the garden walls. A spinning nozzle with a center jet fills the garden with sound and, in summer, an illusion of coolness.

The borders on the four sides of the garden are planted with azaleas and other broadleaf evergreens, a few bulbs and flowers. Several large azaleas are also spotted around the garden in tubs. Almost all bloom comes in the spring. In summer, when the heat is oppressive and gardening is a largely unrewarding chore, the garden is simply a restful green. This color carries over through the winter, thus making the outlook from the rooms above pleasant the year round.

Though in the center of Georgetown, the high-walled garden is remarkably peaceful. Most noticeable sound is of water splashing steadily into pool.

Bricks laid on sand lack rigidity of those in mortar. A few bricks can be lifted out and plants dropped in to bring shadow, shape, and color to the paving.

Mrs. Allen's well-shaded city garden opens wide before you as you step on-
to the porch, but you discover unsuspected features as you walk through it

Garden of

Mrs. Whitney Allen

Rochester, New York

A STATUE commissioned from Gaston Lachaise by Mrs. Allen and the late Mr. Allen dominates her city garden. If you sit where you can see it, you find yourself studying the ever-changing spots of sunlight on its white surface. And if you sit where you can't see it—because it is hidden by the sides of the arch that frames it—the void seems so surprising that you keep worrying over it just as the tip of the tongue keeps worrying over the cavity in a tooth.

Landscape architect Fletcher Steele designed the garden for Mr. and Mrs. Allen in 1916; added the statue about twenty years later. But throughout its long history the garden has rarely stood still. "We try to do something every year," Mrs. Allen says. "We've had to take trees out and put them in. We add bits of sculpture, fountains—right now we're planning for an ornamental iron gate."

Although the garden, which has little color, is so serene that on a warm spring afternoon it almost makes you drowsy, it is remarkably alive. This is undoubtedly attributable in part to the changes that are forever being made. But give credit also to the fact that the garden is not overstuffed in the way that so many gardens of its vintage are. And the sound of running, splashing water is pervasive. There is a tiny fountain next to the porch that sounds like several faucets running into a stoppered basin. And from the base of the statue water spouts a few inches upward and then falls into a semicircular pool from which it spills into a pebbled trough which empties into an ornamental basin which overflows in turn into the small swimming pool.

Mrs. Allen's garden is carefully manicured, and looks it. But gardening in Rochester is not laborious. The fact is that the soil is as fertile and productive as any in the country—maybe more so. And despite the city's latitude, Lake Ontario keeps the temperature from falling to the low figures which annually gain unfavorable publicity for northern New York State.

White statue standing high above the lawn behind elaborate arch dominates Mrs. Allen's garden. Water flows from the base (see opposite page) *into pool.*

One of the garden's surprises is the beech allée *that crosses rear of garden.*
Another (not shown) *is a teahouse like a Saracen's tent made of iron mesh.*

On a clear day, the magnificent lawn running from the Backus house to a wall designed to cut off street sounds opens up view of ships on Lake St. Clair

Garden of

The Late Mr. and Mrs. Standish Backus

Grosse Pointe Shores, Michigan

A GOOD TEST of a garden is whether it is appealing even when without bloom. The Backus garden passes with flying colors. I saw it only a few days after the lilacs—one of Mrs. Backus's specialties—had gone, and while I was regretful, I did not miss them. This is one of the grand gardens of the country—in the grand manner but giving no feeling of being anachronistic—always pleasurable.

Though the property covers about seven acres, it is very narrow in relation to its depth. The huge house is set roughly midway back from the street, which runs along the shore of Lake St. Clair, and is closer to the north boundary than the south. The garden, which was planned by landscape architect Fletcher Steele, of Pittsford, New York, is divided into three main and three subsidiary areas. Directly east of the house, a handsome lawn shaded by large elms slopes ever so slightly down toward the lake. At the end a wall topped with a stone balustrade extends across it like a dam. On the far side, slanting from the top of the solid wall to the street, is a bank of earth taken from the excavation for the house. Its purpose is to shut out street sounds, and it does so very well.

South of the lawn and parallel with it is a wild woodland garden with a long, narrow reflecting pool winding through like an Oriental snake. At any time of the day, this is a pleasant retreat from the more open, adjoining areas.

Directly behind the house, visible from the living rooms, is a smaller lawn and at the back of that a formal pool and a garden stage planted with magnificent boxwood (which has survived the Detroit climate probably only because of the lake's strong tempering influence) and an even more magnificent trimmed hedge of reddish European beeches. Though Mr. and Mrs. Backus may have intended using the stage for

The "long shot," as the Backuses called it, is a long, tapering lawn area with twelve bays filled with lilacs and perennials (see plan on facing page)

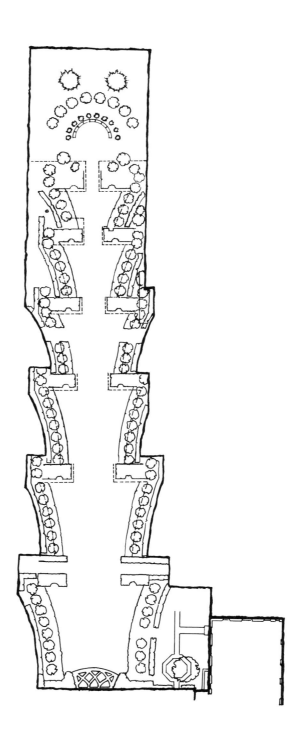

Postscript

"Progress" caught up with Mr. and Mrs. Backus's garden several weeks after this book had reached the point of no return in the production process. The estate was sold; the buyer decided not to move in; and both garden and house were demolished.

All too many of America's outstanding large gardens have met the same fate; and many others are destined to do so unless some satisfactory and fair-to-the-owner way of transferring them to public ownership can be found.

SS

Grape arbor is at right angles to the bayed lawn area and leads into it and across it to cutting garden, where beds are arranged like big stepping stones

dramatics, it never was. It serves the equally good purpose of giving the garden, which is naturally flat, a definite change in elevation.

West of the "stage" garden is the property's most interesting and unusual area. It is a lawn well over 100 yards long and very narrow. Bordered on both sides with trees, tall shrubs, or hedges, it would have offered a fine vista; but Mr. Steele chose to accentuate the vista by arranging the borders in a long, narrow V. The way in which he did

Sandwiched between the front lawn and the neighboring property is a large wooded area through which paths and a streamlike reflecting pool meander

GARDEN OF THE LATE MR. AND MRS. STANDISH BACKUS

this is tricky. Imagine a pine tree with six flat, outstretching branches on one side of the tapering trunk and six matching branches on the exact opposite side of the trunk. This is Mr. Steele's plan for the area, except that he made the branches out of tall arborvitaes.

The branches also serve to divide the garden into twelve bays, six on each side of the lawn. You cannot see what is in these until you are in front of them. So as you stroll from one end of the garden to the other, you are in for a whole series of pleasant surprises. Actually, all twelve bays have a background planting of lilacs; but the perennial borders in front of the lilacs are different from bay to bay.

The beauty of the Backus garden stems mainly from the emphasis on form. Except in the wild garden, everything is placed and shaped with care. The yew hedge between the front lawn and driveway is trimmed in a dentelated fashion that recalls the arborvitae bays bordering the rear lawn. The boxwood mounds around the pool contrast with the high wall formed by the European beeches. The lindens in the same lawn area are like thimbles with straight sides. In the cutting garden tucked to one side of the arborvitae bays, the beds are like huge stepping stones interspersed with apple trees. The grape arbor on the other side of the arborvitae bays has a vaulted roof. The "landing" below the step into the arborvitae area is a Gothic tracery of white stones laid in the grass.

Hedge of European beeches towers behind pool and an untrod, two-level stage floored with grass and edged with box of unusual size for Detroit area

Red roses are the main source of color in the terrace, lawn, and swimming pool area behind the Searles' house. Several materials are used for paving.

Garden of

Mr. and Mrs. John Searle

Lake Forest, Illinois

THE SEARLE GARDEN was only one year old when these pictures were taken. But even at this tender age it displayed a mature elegance that is unusual in gardens of much riper age.

The garden was created by Gertrude E. Kuh, Chicago landscape architect, and her associate, Mary Long Rogers. Their aim was a simple design suitable to a rather formal French house. Their problem—one with which they were thoroughly familiar—was the Chicago area's erratic climate.

The main features of the plan they worked out—the entrance court and the terrace—are the product of Mrs. Kuh's growing interest in paved areas. This interest, in turn, stems from (1) her clients' need for ample parking and outdoor living space and (2) their demand for gardens that are easy to keep up.

The Searles' entrance court is a large square covered with gravel and edged with a three-foot-wide strip of big, round, colorful stones. The strip brings to the area a typically French country look; and it serves the practical purpose of catching the gravel that is pushed to the side by snowplows.

Beyond the court on three sides is an attractive lawn area spotted with apples and native oaks. The stepped terrace across the front of the

Terrace is paved in black slate laid on crushed stone. An upside-down, L-shaped metal edging keeps slates from sliding sideways into plant beds.

Paving in front of house is varied, too. Steps are bluestone; tree circle, cobble-stones; driveway, gravel which is edged with wide strip of big round stones.

*Swimming-pool terrace at end of grass mall is visually cut off from area be-
yond by a low wall. Waving meadow grass brings informality to formal scene.*

house is paved with bluestone and features one sizable maple in the center of a cobblestone circle.

The terrace back of the house is paved with squares and strips of black slate set edge to edge on three inches of crushed limestone. (When Mrs. Kuh makes parking areas of brick or comparable paving blocks, she uses six inches of crushed stone for the base.) Broad steps lead down from here to a mall that is carpeted with Merion bluegrass surrounded by gravel walks. And from there you step down further to the swimming pool centered in a large terrace of concrete with bits of exposed black aggregate.

The whole terrace area is sunswept, formal, and handsome. But it escapes being excessively formal because of the tree-shaded lawns and waving fields around it.

Despite the extent of the entire garden, Mrs. Kuh limited the planting areas mainly to a few large tree, shrub and ground-cover borders next to the driveway and the garages. Her plant list included only the following: *Acer ginnale*, *Euonymus alatus* and *radicans*, Korean box, flowering crabs, apples, hawthorn, yew, mugo pine, honeylocust, native oaks, *Magnolia soulangeana*, pachysandra, and English ivy. For flowers she selected Mrs. Searle's favorite red roses (however, there is also a fine cutting garden at some distance from the house).

Though she is a native of the area, Mrs. Kuh makes no attempt to conceal the difficulties of gardening in and around Chicago. "You have to work hard for about five months of pleasure," she says. "The climate is unpredictable. The soil discourages planting of broadleaf evergreens. Competent help is extremely scarce.

"Because of these problems, we use as little plant material as possible. We don't depend on a garden full of flowers for a successful picture. Rather, we depend more on our lovely flowering trees and shrubs—especially the crabs—and on restful green."

And that, when you come to think of it, does not constitute a very unpleasant horticultural diet for any gardener anywhere. Certainly, in the case of the Searles, it has helped to produce a garden of distinction.

In the Schamberg garden, emphasis is on clean lines, interesting textures, and easy maintenance. Two pieces of sculpture highlight the walled living area.

Garden of

Mr. and Mrs. Morton G. Schamberg

Highland Park, Illinois

FROM THE LARGE, ceiling-high windows of Mr. and Mrs. Schamberg's living room and dining room you look out on their small, wooded hillside garden. It is terraced with Lannon-stone walls and laced with narrow paths. One floor directly below you is a level area covered with carefully raked gravel. Set in the gravel and here and there on the hillside are beautiful rocks of various shapes and colors.

The quiet scene is reminiscent of a Japanese garden. It is chaste, rich with texture and interesting form. It owes its existence to the fact that the Schambergs' property was cut through at this point by a little ravine that had to be shored up with rock walls and partially filled to make it usable. This would have been obvious to anyone. But the idea of finishing it off as it is could have come only from a landscape architect like Gertrude E. Kuh and people with the art interests of the Schambergs.

The rest of the garden is as definitely modern as the house itself. In the large, paved front court, or parking area, the only strong planting pattern is provided by a fine hawthorn and the Virginia creeper trained across the bayed brick walls of the house.

Behind the house, facing a ravine, is the private outdoor living area, consisting of a small lawn and a terrace of cypress blocks. A double

Terrace made of cypress blocks has two focal points: at one side is the lawn area ; at other side is this small arrangement of stones

*Before house was built, this was the upper end of a useless ravine. It is now
a combined rock-and-woodland garden with raked gravel at lowest level.*

Extra-large paved forecourt helps to reduce garden maintenance. Virginia creeper trained on house wall relieves the otherwise stark lines of the area.

Scotch pine rising above an arrangement of variegated stones set in a patch of black gravel borders part of the terrace and forms a handsome focal point.

After I visited the Schambergs' garden (twice), I wondered for some time exactly what it was that made it so effective. I was impressed by its immaculateness (even when I wasn't expected). It harbors a couple of choice sculptures. It makes superb use of striking stones. The plants, though limited in variety, are good specimens well placed. But I finally concluded that the real beauty of the garden lies in its lines. They are simple but ever so fine.

Living room looks out and down on wooded hillside garden, which is partly planted with azaleas. Large stones casually placed have feeling of sculpture.

Mrs. Chandler's garden is tiny but feels surprisingly spacious because it has two distinct parts. This is the larger. The other part is behind holly hedge.

Garden of

Mrs. Warren T. Chandler

St. Louis, Missouri

ONE MOMENT this little garden strikes you as whimsy; the next it seems to make perfect sense.

Right there you have the charm of it. It it gay, fey, and practical all at once.

It was built to give Mrs. Chandler some pleasant outdoor living space with privacy from the neighboring house only a few feet beyond the side boundary. To accomplish this, Perry H. Wheeler, Washington, D.C., landscape architect, built high wood walls on the two open sides of the 22 by 37 foot area (Mrs. Chandler's house forms the other two sides); and projecting inward from these he built a lath roof which is now covered with Concord grapevines. Result: Visually, at least, the house next door has disappeared.

The garden itself is divided into two spaces. Immediately outside the dining room is an open court with a small pool and fountain and assorted bits of sculpture and potted plants. To the left of this, behind a holly hedge, is a larger court, half open to the sky and half roofed. It is partially bordered with scattered shrubs, small trees, and pansies or periwinkles.

Though the layout of the garden is unusual, it could hardly be called unconventional. But the "decoration" is definitely off-beat. For one thing, the diamond-patterned wood treillage with which Mr. Wheeler covered the walls in the small court extends part way into the dining room. Next to the dining room fireplace a statue of a Victorian lady stands in front of a mirrored arch in the trellis.

At the other end of the same court a double door is cut through the trellis. It's a dummy—meant only as a small joke. To give it an extra fillip, Mr. Wheeler stuck a street number on the wall alongside.

In the largest roofed area a ferocious-looking cowardly lion hangs on a wall spitting water into a basin he seems to hold between his paws. He is so completely out of keeping with the Victorian mood of the

Shade and privacy are assured by roof and high wall which, texturally, are in sharp but pleasant contrast with diamond treillage elsewhere in garden

Small court opening off dining room is screened from summer sun by grape-vines trained along wires. Double door to No. 13 is a joke: It doesn't open.

garden that he makes it instantly obvious that the two people most closely connected with the garden—Mrs. Chandler and Mr. Wheeler —are firm believers in getting fun out of life.

Even more whimsical is a bit of sculpture you are not likely to see unless it is pointed out to you. It is an iron rooster—at least twice life size—crowing to the skies from among the grapevines on the roof over the larger court.

I wish that more gardens had a sense of humor like Mrs. Chandler's. It's a refreshing attribute—the more so when you consider how terribly serious most gardens—and gardeners—are.

Could there be any simpler but more enticing garden area than this elm-shaded lawn edged with shrubs and hosta? It adjoins the Andrus driveway.

Garden of

Mr. and Mrs. John E. Andrus, III

Wayzata, Minnesota

TEMPERATURES in the Minneapolis-St. Paul area can soar to 110 in the summer; plummet to minus 40 in the winter. Plants which can withstand such extremes—particularly at the low end of the scale— are not found in huge numbers. But only in the broadleaf evergreen category is the shortage acute.

"But this is our only real problem," says landscape architect Edmund J. Phelps. "And when you get right down to it, it is not a great handicap."

Looking at Mr. and Mrs. Andrus's garden, which Mr. Phelps designed, you must agree. The trees—especially the old elms (Minneapolis has so far not been plagued by the Dutch elm disease)—are handsome. There is fine variety in the shrubs. The ninebark hedge bordering the back lawn and the flower and shrubbery borders is tight and trim. The roses, perennials, and annuals are collectively as lovely as you could ask for. And the lawn, though widely shaded, is excellent: Testimony to the fact that lawn-making and upkeep in this area are easy. You don't even need fertilizer!

A long apple orchard to the right rear of the house provides the axis for the principal garden area. Standing at the end of this, you look down through a wide *allée* of mixed shrubs and peonies; across the

Allée of mixed shrubs and peonies forms part of the axis for the principal garden area. Excellent perennial border (also shown right) *is in distance.*

back lawn, which is like a huge terrace overlooking an open field and tennis court; and down the perennial border to the rounded shrubs that seal the end. It is a pleasant, colorful vista.

The rose garden forms three-quarters of a circle to the left of the perennial border and just off the small paved terrace and dining room. It has an intimate, cohesive look that is, for some reason, often lacking in rose gardens.

Another large lawn area is to the right of the driveway and the house. It is one of the prettiest parts of the garden though it consists of nothing more than grass, elms, and a fine edging of hosta inside a shrub border.

When I asked Mr. Phelps what his objectives were in planning the garden, he answered first: "To have a *comfortable* design." This is not an adjective that is often applied to gardens, but there is no reason why comfort in the garden is not as valid an idea as comfort in the home. In any event, comfortable is a good word for the Andrus garden.

From terrace set into a corner of the house you have a view of perennial bor-
der, rose garden (left of chair), and open space beyond lawn (right of tree)

Though the Andrus garden has a comfortable air that invites you to relax and enjoy life, it has a quiet distinction that discourages sloppiness by the user

Rose garden can be enjoyed from and is within easy reach of other parts of the garden and the house. Yet it has a look of separateness and intimacy.

*A study in contrasts: the formal, parklike lawn areas immediately behind
Mrs. Halpin's house, and the scrub woods and glistening lake in the distance*

Garden of

Mrs. George H. Halpin

Wayzata, Minnesota

PART OF MRS. HALPIN'S GARDEN is a park with rolling lawns, fine trees, and glistening Lake Minnetonka in the background. The rest of the garden is very clipped, genteel, formal—and beautiful.

This was the third large, formal garden I visited, and much the youngest. It was developed in 1951, a time when the country was rapidly turning its back on formality and tradition. But Mrs. Halpin's garden was, to me, the clinching evidence that back-turning was a mistake. I am all in favor of informal, modern, and contemporary gardens; but let's also have the more formal traditional gardens—provided, of course, they are as effective as this.

The garden grows on you the longer you are in it. There is much to enjoy. The perennial garden and the rose garden on either side of an arborvitae *allée*. The former is more or less circular on the perimeter; but the wide grass path through it is shaped like a three-leaf clover with a daintily curving petiole. In the center of this is a small round pool and fountain. The surrounding border is planted with old favorites, including handsome delphiniums, which do especially well in the Minneapolis area.

The rose garden is simpler but nonetheless lovely. It is set between a screened garden house and a semicircle of trimmed arborvitae backed with taller spruces.

The rose garden is one of several distinct but not isolated garden areas. Garden house at left separates the garden from the main house and rear lawn.

The *allée* leads from the dining room to a tall fountain. The area is entirely green and white—the latter being provided by four large stone urns and a succession of white flowers: peonies, phlox, dahlias, etc.

Carefully clipped shrubs and trees—mostly evergreens but including a few deciduous species—are also planted in the great entrance court and on the upper and lower terraces overlooking the lake. The court, with its slim green cones, pincushions, and wheels set against a dense, curving hedge is especially reminiscent of the old formal gardens of France.

Edmund J. Phelps, landscape architect, designed the garden with the help of his associates, Louise P. Mealey and Mrs. Kenneth Hansing.

And he is still at it. Just a while ago, when Mrs. Halpin decided it was time to do something new, he started converting a small woods on the property into a wild woodland garden. It is, of course, totally different from the older parts of the garden—a fact which adds to your enjoyment of *all* parts. But don't take this to mean that the formal areas need a foil to bring you pleasure: They are quite capable of doing this all by themselves.

Arborvitae allée *visible from dining room is very formal and has a green and white color scheme that is relieved only by the sky and the bluish spruces*

Strong vertical lines of the chimney are repeated by the arborvitaes. Horizontal lines of bricks and shingles are accented by other foundation plants.

On other side of entrance court, the stiffly trimmed evergreens, statues, and benches set against a dense curving hedge recall formal gardens of France

Perennial garden is more or less circular, but the path is shaped like a clover.
The stem of the clover is edged with yews; the leaves, with pink petunias.

*The Bennings' classic pool contrasts sharply with mountains. The house,
some distance to the left, is reached via the narrow steps or the broad lawn.*

Garden of

Mr. and Mrs. Arthur E. Benning

Ogden, Utah

WHEN THE BENNINGS BUILT their house in the mid-fifties, they had a well worked-out plan for landscaping the entire place. But lack of water (the area gets only about 14 inches of precipitation a year) prevented them from going beyond construction of the driveway and terrace. Then, in 1960, when ample irrigation water at last became available, they decided to make a new start with the help of Thomas D. Church, San Francisco landscape architect.

"Our objectives were pretty simple," Mr. Benning says. "We wanted a garden compatible with our country site and that would be equally pleasing in the heat of summer and the snow of winter and during the other awful times of the year."

This is precisely what Mr. Church gave them—and without making drastic changes in the original plan. Despite the paucity of plants which do well in this arid, rocky area with temperatures that have swung between minus 30 and 107, the Bennings' garden has the clean, simple lines and texture that make it a year-round pleasure.

A pleasanter terrace with a more dramatic outlook is hard to imagine. The huge paving blocks of exposed aggregate sweep around the living-room wing of the house. At one end of the terrace, a broad flight of steps made of native stone leads up to a small lawn area with a flower and shrub border at the rear and behind that, looming high above, a mountain. At the side of the terrace and level with it a much larger lawn leads away to a more distant view.

But if the terrace is a delight that imparts an air of excitement, the swimming pool area is an excitement that proves a never-ending delight. This is without doubt one of Mr. Church's best pools—and that is saying a lot, because his pools are magnificent.

It is situated at some distance from the house in a cluster of native scrub oaks so that it will not be visible in winter. It can be approached either by a walk through the oaks or by circling around the oaks on the big lawn just mentioned. When you come upon it for the first time, you are stopped dead in your tracks.

Here in this wild, rugged country is a man-made gem of most classic but simple lines: a perfectly round pool set in the center of an octagonal terrace of unpolished terrazzo with a parapet seat wall on seven sides and a wonderfully open, light-as-air-looking pavillion on the eighth.

When I asked Mr. Church the reason for this surprising design, he answered: "The plan was suggested by the lay of the land. I recessed the pool—dropped it somewhat below the lawn level—because in situations like this there is often an embarrassment between the natural land and what you're doing. Here we were trying to get a break between land and pool. I wanted at all costs to avoid any attempt to collaborate with nature."

Terrace of exposed aggregate poured in big squares edged with redwood sweeps around clump of trees. Behind camera is a flower and shrub border.

Round pool is in center of an octagonal terrace with a parapet seat wall that seems to rest high in treetops. Pavilion of modern-classic design is at right.

Both in the woods and in the open, Mrs. Miller has carpeted the ground with an incredible array of plants arranged as she has seen them growing in nature

Garden of

Mr. and Mrs. Pendleton Miller

Seattle, Washington

MR. AND MRS. MILLER'S GARDEN was fifteen years old in 1966. It was not finished. It may never be finished because Mrs. Miller is not one to rest on her gardening laurels. But even if it were only one-fourth or one-tenth its present size, it would be an exceptional garden.

Mrs. Miller is inclined to give the credit for its beauty to the natural setting on a forested hill overlooking Puget Sound and the snow-capped Olympic Mountains beyond. But even without this majestic backdrop the garden wins high honors for design and highest honors for plant material.

The landscape architect was John W. Fischer. His plan is informal in the extreme—in keeping with Mrs. Miller's interests. He made no attempt to compete with the view. Near the street, the garden is a well-planted woodland which gradually thins out as you descend to the house. Behind the house, which is fringed all the way round with delightful borders and terraces, the steep, terraced land is open for about a hundred yards; then a line of tall trees spears upward to accent the distant view. Below these the land drops off sharply to the water.

Except for a few strips of lawn and the more distant downhill area, the garden is cultivated with an intensity that you rarely see. But it is anything but fussy. Mrs. Miller long ago developed an "insatiable curiosity" about the cultivation of plants. She is especially interested in determining which out-of-the-ordinary species will grow in the Seattle area and why. As a result, she collects plants from around the world; at latest count had over four hundred genera with over fifteen hundred species and varieties. They range from tropical specimens to those found in the Arctic (a fact which indicates that the Puget Sound region supports the widest assortment of plant life of any part of the country). A few are not grown successfully anywhere else in the United States.

How does Mrs. Miller attain the results she does—brilliant spring and fall color, wonderful year-round texture, and no end of interest for both novice and expert gardener? By studying how plants grow in nature and then attempting to duplicate nature's ways. Here are some of the observations she made on this score in a talk before the Seattle Garden Club several years ago. I give them in the order she did:

"Plants that are normally covered by snow in winter can succeed in areas where the rainfall is heavy in winter provided they are situated on a steep bank or given the overhead protection of conifer branches so that they won't be beaten down by hammering rains.

"It is not advisable to give the added protection of shade to alpine plant material when planted in the lowlands. Such protection usually promotes overly lush growth, which lessens the strength of the flowers, weakens the plant's basic structure, and shortens its life. The plant seems to have a better chance if grown in the open, fully exposed, with protection provided by numbers of plants—preferably of its own kind, for effect. Otherwise, surround the plant with companion plants suitable in relationship, prostrate ground covers or, better still, sun-loving moss which provides the necessary humidity.

"In observing plants growing in full sun at high altitudes, note that even though the surface of the rocks may be blistering, the bottom side of the rocks and the soil underneath are cool and moist. This is not true in the lowlands. In full sun, shallow rocks heat all the way through and the ground itself cooks down to appreciable depth. The soil can be kept cool if the rocks are imbedded with the least possible amount of surface exposed. Rotten wood also serves the same purpose and is particularly good in retaining moisture if underneath the soil surface. To combine the two is to have everything!

Breathtaking view of Puget Sound adds to beauty of garden, but plants are not placed to benefit by or compete with it. They speak for themselves.

GARDEN OF MR. AND MRS. PENDLETON MILLER

Even in a foundation border near front door Mrs. Miller uses chunks of rotten wood and stones to reproduce natural conditions under which plants grow

"During the time that a plant is becoming established in an open exposure it is particularly important that it not be given fertilizers. This is likely to force rapid growth and shorten the life of the plant.

"Success or failure with plants depends basically on whether sufficient drainage has been provided through the addition of rock and peat to the soil. Crushed gravel, incidentally, is better than pea gravel because the soil washes down through the latter and can easily form the equivalent of concrete.

"In viewing plants in their native habitat, you see that every plant seems to be growing out of another. Consequently, a plant whose main stem is coming out of bare ground looks naked and in need of a cloak. This brings up the use of ground covers, which serve several purposes. First, you will notice that during a freeze a plant coming out of bare soil suffers more. This is because the changes in temperature are so acute above and below the soil line. With a ground cover around the plant, the difference in temperature from the top of the plant to the roots is more gradual and the plant has more time to adjust. Ground covers also keep the soil shaded during hot weather, when the plant is adjusting to the extremes of temperature. Also during hot weather, if a plant has no ground cover, watering can chill the roots and force new growth. Granted that a plant without a ground cover has to be watered to be kept alive; however, this same plant can survive the heat without water if given the protection of ground covers.

"Moles are sometimes bad citizens; but I have found that if I use ground covers with a tight, netted web of roots, the moles and other burrowing animals are inclined to keep their runs well below the surface of the soil. Thus they provide underground drainage—and do my cultivating for me.

"There are many plants native to alkaline conditions at all altitudes. Some people think that, inasmuch as this is their native habitat, you must create the same conditions in your garden. I have had the opposite experience, and believe that in areas where lime is prevalent there are many other accompanying factors that are equally important. If you use lime with the accompanying factors absent, the plants may survive; but I have found that by growing the same plants—some with and some without lime—the plants without lime adjusted to our conditions and did better than those given it.

"A plant can be in full shade adjacent to a surface that reflects sun, and it will receive as much light as if it were out in the open.

"When setting out plants, if you take pains to give them the exposure, soil, drainage, ground covers, etc., that they need—*and then leave them alone*—you will find that they learn to take care of themselves and do well. And your maintenance problems from then on will be greatly minimized."

In Mrs. Roth's unparalleled garden there are big vistas and little vistas. This little one is across the garden from the formal area. Wisteria is everywhere.

Garden of

Mrs. William P. Roth

San Mateo, California

Mrs. ROTH'S GARDEN is a collection of exquisite gems formed into a superb brooch. It is so many-faceted that you must see it again and again to discover all its secrets. Yet its magnificence overwhelms you at first sight.

Development of the garden, which covers about twelve acres, was started in 1915. The owners at that time were the late Mr. and Mrs. William B. Bourn. The Bourns were Irish, and apparently they saw in the San Mateo Valley where they settled something of their homeland. In any event, the garden they created was like the great formal English gardens of that period. It remains this today.

Surprisingly, the garden—really a series of gardens—does not lie directly behind the brick mansion so that it can be easily viewed from indoors. It is centered instead on the Georgian clock tower surmounting the garage, which is hidden behind one of the garden's many brick walls. In back of the tower is an open, sunken garden; and behind that, stretching toward the wooded western hills, are two double rows of tall English yews flanking a smooth sweep of lawn and the swimming pool. To the right of the sunken garden and raised a few feet above it is the live-oak-shaded terrace behind the house; to the left, behind a high wall, is the formal garden, which is subdivided into smaller,

The sunken garden is behind garage. Beyond the high hedge is a wide lawn and a swimming pool—the whole area flanked by two double rows of yews.

hedge-bordered gardens and lawn areas. To the left of this, in turn, is the cutting garden, also formally laid out. Although each of these main elements is separate and distinct, all are held together by vistas down the straight walks and by the dark, flat-topped yews that can be seen rising above the walls and hedges in various parts of the garden.

The yews are unquestionably the principal accent. Even in the formal garden, where they compete for attention with other trees, they stand out. Some are more or less solitary sentinels; most are in phalanxes, leading the eye to the hills or a little pool.

But dominating everything—even the yews—are the great trees. They are magnificent—the live oaks and Italian stone pines especially. Perhaps better than anything else, they indicate what a benign climate the San Francisco peninsula has. Provided that you break up and condition the heavy adobe soil that is often encountered, and provided also that you give plenty of water, you can grow almost anything superlatively.

Mrs. Roth takes advantage of this fact. Her plant list is extensive and includes many exotics. But even the common plants get superb care. Emphasis is always on growing perfect specimens. One of the gardeners who came upon me photographing a brilliant bed of excel-

Another view of sunken garden, which, like all other parts of Mrs. Roth's vast garden, has frequent changes of raiment. House is to right on a higher level.

lent cinerarias pooh-poohed the plants when I praised them. "They're nothing. We'll be pulling them out in a week," he said. Then he led me to a nearby hedge of English holly—as shiny and tight and carefully clipped as any hedge I ever saw. This, he indicated by a few gestures, was the way plants grown at Filoli—the name of Mrs. Roth's home—are really supposed to be.

The moral is obvious: When you have a beautiful garden to start with and superimpose on it a perfectionist attitude and a salubrious climate, a great garden is bound to result. This one is exactly that.

Terrace behind house dances with shadows cast by live oaks. On this side, house is partly swathed in an immense wisteria vine that perfumes the air.

The different views across the tremendous formal garden are too numerous to count; but like this one, all are filled with grass, color, and English yews

The Brookes' pool not only dominates the garden but is the garden; yet it is so placed, designed, and planted around that it seems part of natural scene

Garden of

Mr. and Mrs. John Brooke

Woodside, California

TODAY'S SWIMMING POOLS, with their intensely colored, sparkling water, are not easy to subdue visually. Partly for this reason, many homeowners make them the principal feature of the garden.

The Brookes' pool is exactly that. Indeed, you might say that the pool area is the whole garden, for there is relatively little planned planting elsewhere (Mr. and Mrs. Brooke wanted their house to blend smoothly with the surrounding woods). Yet despite the fact that the pool insists on calling itself to your attention, it does not introduce an alien note into the over-all natural scene.

This is rather amazing when you consider several points: First of all, you look down on the pool from most parts of the house; therefore, the expanse of water you see seems large. Second, the pool is a circle— and anything so geometrical usually seems out of phase with nature. Third, it has a wide, sunny paved area half way around it. Finally, the white awning covering part of the terrace contrasts sharply with the green of the water and green of the trees. (The awning was not originally planned for, but had to be added when the sun's heat turned out to be more of a problem than had been expected.)

Added together, these four points should theoretically give the pool an out-of-place look. But it actually looks quietly natural.

Large, flat rocks scattered around the pool rim have the feeling of sculptured seals basking in the sun. They help to tie the pool into rock-strewn hillside.

From an unseen source in the heavily planted hillside, water splashes down over rocks into the pool. The small scene is more real than nature itself.

Looking down from the house to the pool, which lies blue and quiet in midst of towering trees. From the pool there is a view of a wooded hill far to left.

The trees in the background are one of the reasons for this. They loom high over the pool in the same way that tall pines ring a mountain pond. At one point, where a few of them have been cut away, a wooded hill in the distance moves in upon the scene.

The planting that landscape architect Thomas D. Church planned for the hillside between the pool and the terrace off the back of the house is another reason for the pool's natural look. It is far more varied than in nature, but the shrubs, ferns, and small trees are so casually placed and intermingle so pleasantly that the slope appears to be "just right." Furthermore, when you are sitting on the terrace, some of the taller plants get in the way of the view of the pool and thus change the smooth, circular outline.

Last of all are the rocks—big flat rocks that Mr. Church placed on the hillside and scattered here and there around the flat pool rim. Some form the basis for the waterfall that splashes down from the hill into the pool. Some are steps leading to the higher terrace. Those resting on the terrace around the pool help to unify pool and hillside and change the lines of the pool rim. Several of the rocks also have the feeling of sculpture.

Most people call the Brookes' garden informal. Mr. Church considers it pretty formal. His theory is that it is not necessary for the *pool* to be informal, but that the people in the composition *feel* informal. Whatever the facts, the garden is uncommonly delightful.

Broad walk to the Grants' front door (unseen far to left) *from the parking area* (behind top steps) *is indirect and partly shaded by big, high pergola*

Garden of
Mr. and Mrs. Spencer Grant
Hillsborough, California

O N A BRIGHT SUMMER DAY Mr. and Mrs. Grant's garden carries one clear and compelling message: "Enjoy life." The garden offers many ways to do it.

You can float in the blue, shade-dappled swimming pool; play on the sweeping lawn that is shadowed here and there by live oaks; relax on the open terrace or under the protection of the pergola; cool yourself in the breezes flowing through the open glass doors of the octagonal gazebo; contemplate the tiny man-made brook that tumbles out of a wooded hill, over rocks, into pools, and through crooked sluiceways into the swimming pool; enjoy the beauty and fragrance of the flowering plants massed between the pergola and the children's play yard.

The Grants' garden, in short, is as full of inviting, informal but well-polished charm as a garden can be. It got that way through careful planning by the owners, their architect, and landscape architect Lawrence Halprin in collaboration.

In the San Francisco Bay area, more than in any other part of the country, steep hills present a challenge to the home builder and gardener. The acreage the Grants selected for their new home was not so steep as many plots but it had enough slope to create problems. For

Undulating pool lies well below gazebo (unseen to right) *and above magnificent lawn. Recirculated water burbles out of wooded hillside behind camera.*

one thing, the house was very large and would not rest comfortably on the hillside unless special measures were taken. For another thing, Mr. and Mrs. Grant wanted their children to have plenty of space for play.

The solution that was evolved was to set the house lengthwise on a two-level terrace built across the breast of the hill. Both tiers are supported by long, stone-masonry walls. The upper tier, which is paved and used as the main living terrace, extends eastward across the hill to the gazebo. The stone wall supporting the tier and the pergola running to the gazebo link the gazebo visually with the house. The effect, as Mr. Halprin says, is to seat the buildings in a relaxed attitude on the hillside. The steepness of the slope is also minimized.

Below the terrace lie the magnificent lawn and swimming pool. Though slightly undulating and interrupted here and there with spreading trees, the lawn provides the youngsters with an excellent playing field. When I asked Mr. Grant how he maintained it, he wrote: "Of course, you realize that a Bay area lawn has to be seeded only once, since our winters are not severe. The seed we used was a mixture of perennial rye, creeping red fescue and Kentucky bluegrass. We feed the lawn three times a year—in early spring, summer and late fall— with a slow-release, high-nitrogen fertilizer. We have found that if we cut the lawn very short in winter, it discourages mold or other fungi; and we purposely leave it long in summer. Watering is done as needed."

The inviting swimming pool, despite its carefully sculptured appearance, achieves an unusual naturalness from the fact that its edges flow in and out around a group of ancient overhanging oaks and a small rock garden descending from the gazebo.

Although the green of the lawn, the brown of the house, and the blue of the pool dominate the color scheme, Mr. and Mrs. Grant have brightened the scene with innumerable flowering plants. Wisteria drips from the pergolas (there is also a large one over the front walk). Rhododendrons are massed in a grove of trees at the street end of the lawn. Primroses are planted around another group of trees at the middle of the lawn. Azaleas are tucked into the rock garden near the gazebo and under a live oak at the house end of the pergola. Leptospermum and other colorful shrubs and flowers border the pergola on the uphill side. Orchids in large pots ring the gazebo.

House and garden are in perfect harmony because they were planned togeth-er from the start. The house (this is one end of it) sits sideways on hillside.

Orchids grow under the gazebo's partially open roof extension, and pink lep-
tospermum, and other colorful shrubs border the wisteria-drenched pergola

*In contrast with the straight lines of the McCulloughs' house, the rear terrace
moves in big, rounded waves under the roof overhang and out into the lawn*

Garden of

Mr. and Mrs. Jack A. McCullough

Los Altos Hills, California

M R. AND MRS. MC CULLOUGH'S HOUSE sits atop a steep hill. From the front there is an immense view across the southern end of San Francisco Bay. From the back there is a not quite so immense, more pleasurable view across a valley to wooded hills. Understandably, one of the McCulloughs' objectives—which was shared by Robert Royston of the landscape architectural firm of Royston, Hanamoto, Mayes and Beck—was to design the garden so that both views could be enjoyed to the fullest.

A second objective was to have a garden that could be easily maintained.

A third objective—which originated with Mr. Royston—was to "work with spaces and shapes that were complementary to the low, long, rectilinear house."

If you climb the little rise at the swimming pool end of the house you can tell in an instant how well the three objectives have been attained. You are also struck by a feeling that this is a delightfully different kind of garden. It has clean, modern lines; is very architectural— much larger than it appears from any given point; and is extremely open and sunny.

Main aim of the garden design was to bring in the views; consequently, the planting in the rear is low, but a few trees are used to give scale and accent

Long, flat rear lawn is cut partly in two by a slightly elevated border. The area on the far side is flooded with sun; on this side, scattered trees give shade.

GARDEN OF MR. AND MRS. JACK A. MCCULLOUGH   133

The sweeping terrace projects right into the living area of the house. It is screened from sun by wide louvers and is crossed by a still, moatlike pool.

The land is flat except for two slight mounds which Mr. Royston built to give a sense of enclosure to one section of the covered terrace. The outer edge of the lawn—where the land falls off to the deep valley below—sweeps in a long, graceful, compound curve in contrast to the straight lines of the house. The paved terrace also loops in and out from under the overhanging roof of the house. One big loop extends far out and encompasses the swimming pool. Another smaller loop runs more or less parallel with the house and includes a planting pocket. Yet another loop is perpendicular to the house and unadorned.

The garden's only real planting strip is a boomerang-shaped peninsula extending out from the house across the lawn at its widest point. Planted with a few small trees, shrubs, and clumps of flowers, it appears from a distance to cut right across the long lawn. Closer up, however, you find that the lawn actually flows around it as an ocean current sweeps around a jetty.

Among other things, the peninsula divides the lawn into two "climate" zones. The larger zone, outside the living and utility areas of the house, is wide open and sun-drenched. There are only four small trees to break the view from the terrace, and they seem insignificant against the vast panorama of green ridges and blue sky. Here children and grandchildren can run and play ball and loll beside the pool to heart's content. The smaller lawn area outside the bedroom wing has a number of fairly sizable trees. Though the lawn here is also bright with sun, the shadows of the trees—shadows that move with the breezes—give an illusion of widespread shade that encourages croquet-playing, reading, and just sitting and listening to the birds in an old oak tree.

*Cornerstone of the McIntyres' modern Moorish water garden is this large,
thick fountain. The sound of it helps make you feel cool even under hot sun.*

Garden of

Mr. and Mrs. Henry McIntyre

Hillsborough, California

S OME GARDENS INVITE NAMING. This is one of them. But it defies naming, too. If I called it a concrete garden, you would be appalled at the picture that came to mind. If I called it a water garden, you would probably think of a garden built around and into a lake. If I called it a modern Moorish garden, you would know what I meant if you had traveled abroad. Yet all these names are accurate.

Mr. and Mrs. McIntyre became entranced with Moorish water gardens during their visits to Spain. When they set out to build a new house in Hillsborough several years ago, they asked landscape architect Lawrence Halprin to explore the idea of developing a similar garden. A not-unimportant reason for their interest was their hope of having a garden that did not require a great deal of maintenance.

"The McIntyres hit us at just the right time," Mr. Halprin recalls. "It happened that we had been thinking along much the same line. We were interested in outdoor space as a cultural event. We were interested in the use of water. And we were interested in gardens that are evocative to the people in them—but not because of their flowers. We worked closely with the McIntyres' architect, and the plan we eventually came up with suited the McIntyres almost exactly."

The magical effect of Mr. and Mrs. McIntyre's unlikely garden, with its 90 degree angles and flat, gray concrete surfaces, is traceable to a a subtle combination of things.

No matter from where it is viewed—from inside the house, from the top of the surrounding hill, from the island in its center—the garden has a strong sculptural feeling.

It is filled with actual movement: water moving at various speeds; waving shadows cast by the eucalyptus trees that form towering hedges to east and west; the foliage of the few plants that are in the

Even at 3 P.M. (when this picture was taken), the sun is sliding behind the tall eucalyptus trees and the stiff, white garden fills with moving shadows

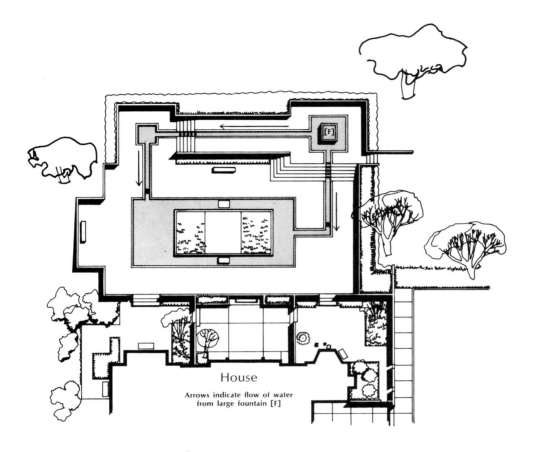

House

Arrows indicate flow of water
from large fountain [F]

garden blowing in the breeze; birds coming for a drink or a bath. All this seems more apparent than in the usual garden because the background is so still.

The sound of water fills the air; and the tune changes as you walk from one part of the garden to the other and as the wind changes force. (The tune can also be changed by operating the fountains alone or in pairs instead of all three at once.) The large, thick fountain—the cornerstone of the water system—gives off a continuous, modulated roar. The steps down which the water tumbles in two directions from the big fountain are scooped out to produce a gurgling sound. The tall, single spout splashes irregularly into the pool below while the three small sprays patter like rain.

The end result of the garden's sounds and movement and sculptural qualities is somewhat surprising. At first sight, you are filled with excitement. Then this abates (but never totally disappears) to be replaced by a feeling of peace—clean and uncluttered.

*The beauty of the high, white, angular walls is accented by the flat, green is-
land. Blocks in channel change the movement and sound of the flowing water.*

Hillside directly behind garden (and at both ends) is planted only to meadow grass. In the channel the steps are undercut to give water a gurgling sound.

Brilliance of the ice plants that carpet the hill outside Mrs. Miller's bedroom
is accented by the rugged ranch country that stretches northward for miles

Garden of

Mrs. Hortense Miller

Laguna Beach, California

WHEN MRS. MILLER MOVED to southern California fourteen years ago, she knew that gardening would be far easier than she had known it to be in the Midwest. But she underestimated the difference. Even today she is amazed by five things:

1. The range of plants that she can grow seems infinite. They include not only many of the species she has known since childhood but also an enormous assortment from California and the Southwest, Australia, South Africa, and Central and South America. A list of the varieties that were *in bloom* in her garden on March 2, 1965, gives a partial idea of what she can and does grow:

Abutilon	Blue-eyed grass
Acacia	Bottlebrush (2 kinds)
African daisy (6 kinds)	Breath-of-heaven
Ageratum	*Bryophyllum* (2 kinds)
Allium	Buckwheat
Aloe	Cactus
Alyssum	Calamondin
Amaryllis	California poppy
Apricot	*Calliandra*
Azalea (2 kinds)	*Camellia* (3 kinds)
Begonia	Carnation

Castilleja

Cerastium

Christmas cactus

Cistus

Clivia

Coral bell

Coral tree

Corokia

Crassula (3 kinds)

Cuphea

Cymbidium

Daylily (3 kinds)

Echeveria

Echium

Encelia

Epidendrum

Eucalyptus (2 kinds)

Freesia

Fremontia

Forget-me-not

Fuchsia

Geranium (8 kinds)

Gladiolus

Grape hyacinth

Graptopetalum

Hellebore (2 kinds)

Hyacinth

Iris (3 kinds)

Jasmine (2 kinds)

Johnny-jump-up (2 kinds)

Kalanchoe (2 kinds)

Kenilworth ivy

Lampranthus

Lemonadeberry

Leptospermum (2 kinds)

Lime

Lobelia

Lotus

Madrone

Mallow

Marguerite (3 kinds)

Mazus

Mesembryanthemum (8 kinds)

Mimulus

Morning glory

Narcissus (4 kinds)

Nasturtium

Nightshade

Ochna

Orange (2 kinds)

Ornithogalum

Oxalis (3 kinds)

Pansy

Patience

Pentstemon

Pinks

Pittosporum

Polygonum

Potentilla

Primrose

Raphiolepis

Ribes (3 kinds)

Rockrose

Rose (3 kinds)

Rosemary (2 kinds)

Rue

Sedum

Sparaxis

Squill

Stock

Streptosolen

Sunrose

Thyme (2 kinds)

Triteleia

Trychospermum

Tulbaghia

Tulip

Verbena (3 kinds)

Viburnum

Vinca

Wintersweet

Wisteria

Yesterday-today-and-tomorrow

TOTAL: 157 varieties

2. There is no season of the year when Mrs. Miller does not have bloom; and some plants such as solanum, agathea, geraniums, pentstemon, marguerites, and mesembyranthemum bloom almost all year.

*A feature of the parking area is this ancient, wind-torn tree planted with suc-
culents that are here being water-misted from concealed nozzles and tubes*

Even in dark December and January she has counted ninety different varieties in bloom.

3. The death rate of plants, other than annuals, tulips, and hyacinths, is almost zero. (Of course, there are a number of cold-needing plants that would die if planted.)

4. Plants in southern California grow right up to the trunks of trees; and there is no problem about keeping many varieties alive and happy on the north side of a building.

5. The fragrance of a California garden, whether the day is sunny or rainy, is in Mrs. Miller's words, "wonderful."

Given such favored gardening conditions, even an ordinary gardener should be successful in southern California. But Mrs. Miller is more than an ordinary gardener.

Her house is built high into the side of a precipitous hill overlooking the Pacific Ocean to the west and other steep hills to the north. The latter are open—the property of an immense ranch. The canyon far below Mrs. Miller's windows is lined with feathery grass, usually brown, chapparal, and yellow sandstone outcroppings that are pockmarked with holes. It is rather typical California-seaside country.

Mrs. Miller owns two and one-third acres. She presently cultivates about half of this. The garden is extraordinary. As she and her landscape gardener, Donald Estep, designed it, it not only surrounds the house but extends right into it in several places. It is essentially a number of small gardens, each rather intimate and with its own personality, but all flowing together to form a whole. Even the largest garden area—on the hillside below the house—is laid out in this fashion. Viewed either from the top or the bottom of the hill, it seems unified. But when you walk through it, you find that the placement of plants and the zigzagging of the bark-covered paths divide it into several gardens, all with their own little vistas or points of interest.

Thus, while the entire garden has great serenity, it also invokes a sense of discovery. You seem forever to be coming on something new, something that excites, something that makes you pause.

But the design of Mrs. Miller's garden is not the sole reason for its exciting charm. As the preceding plant list indicates, it is horticulturally exceptional. Private gardens simply do not display such variety. Nor do they, as a rule, display their wares so satisfyingly. Somehow, despite the multiplicity of varieties Mrs. Miller and Mr. Estep have

*Not content simply to grow a huge collection of gorgeous plants, Mrs. Miller
and Mr. Estep spend much time training some of them, as in entrance court*

GARDEN OF MRS. HORTENSE MILLER 147

planted, they have avoided hodgepodge. On the contrary, even when many different varieties crowd close together, there is a feeling of unity.

Such perfection—though owing much to what Mrs. Miller calls "this gentle land"—is not achieved without some problems.

The worst of these are the deer, which descend from the surrounding hills to feed on everything from dainty flowers to the bark of the Torrey pines. Because of them, Mrs. Miller has been forced to enclose part of the garden with high bamboo and wire fences.

Other problems are the wind, which occasionally roars down through the canyon, upsetting trees, and the never-ending need for

Unique gazebo overlooking the largest terrace, the house, and the Pacific Ocean is reached by steps curving up hillside planted with Zoysia tenuifolia

Terrace with louvered roof is cage for two white cockatoos. White alyssum and pink begonias tie in with blue, red, and white paintings by Mrs. Miller.

cleaning up. "In the Midwest we cleaned up in spring and fall," Mrs. Miller says. "Here it's a year-round occupation."

Soil is thin throughout the southern California coastal area and especially where the land has been chiseled away, as in Mrs. Miller's case, to form the site for a house. The solution is to mix in redwood sawdust or peat, both of which help to offset the alkalinity of the soil in addition to building up its humus content. Also needed is fertilizer in quantity. Mr. Estep uses a nitrogen-rich liquid.

Finally, there is the watering problem. As Mrs. Miller's garden has grown, the underground sprinkling system has grown with it. Sprinkler heads and hoses are everywhere. A pump is needed to raise the water pressure. But the actual use of water is not so great as the elaborate system implies. Some plants, to be sure, need to be watered daily. But most require only a three-hour soaking once every couple of weeks.

Mr. Eckbo's garden is a closely related series of living areas created with
aluminum panels. The wall here is a one-way screen of brown and gold mesh.

Garden of

Mr. and Mrs. Garrett Eckbo

Los Angeles, California

M R. ECKBO IS A PARTNER of the landscape architectural firm of Eckbo, Dean, Austin & Williams. He believes that one aim of landscape design is "to establish an integrated relationship between man-made elements and natural forms."

In 1952, when Mr. and Mrs. Eckbo moved into their new modern home in the Hollywood Hills, the level part of their half-acre lot was raw, compacted fill with hardly a weed and blazing hot. Eight years later, when the Aluminum Company of America commissioned Mr. Eckbo to design a number of outdoor aluminum structures, the garden —through Mr. Eckbo's manual efforts—had become lush with vegetation. "This was essential to the successful use of so much metal in the garden," Mr. Eckbo recalls. "Without it, the metal would have been too thin, hard and frivolous. But with it, it becomes rich and elegant."

The structures Mr. Eckbo developed include two large shelters, various screens, and a fountain. All but the last are made of thin aluminum which is expanded to create perforated, plaster-lathlike sheets of tiny louvers. The purpose of the shelters—one attached to the house; the other free-standing—is to dilute and filter the harsh southern California sun. The screens all serve as partial space dividers and also as one-way vision controls. Mr. Eckbo feels that as residential properties

Fanciful garden house consists of a corrugated roof made of aluminum mesh and front and rear aluminum screens, all supported on a dark redwood frame

Curved fence at end of terrace is assembled from aluminum panels of varying widths and of four subtle textures. They have gold or yellow anodized finish.

become smaller and as families spend more time outdoors, the need becomes greater for subdivision of the garden space in order to give a feeling of greater size and wonder.

The two structures face each other across the lawn. Between them, at one end of the lawn, is the fountain. It is made of heavy aluminum plate and finished in gray-green enamel. The water outlets are five tubes resembling the stamens of a flower. Water overflows from the fountain into a curved concrete basin in which several large, rough rocks are arranged. The whole design is a splendid example of what Mr. Eckbo means when he talks about integration of man-made elements and natural forms.

Use of so much metal was possible only because of garden's vegetation. Roof here is a sun break in which flat brown panels alternate with gold pyramids.

Fountain is an abstract flower made of heavy aluminum plate enameled gray-green. Stamens are natural aluminum color. Fountain is about six feet wide.

A gorgeous thicket of bougainvillea and allamanda borders driveway (unseen to left) sweeping down to clipped lawn area surrounding Mrs. Roth's house

Garden of

Mrs. William P. Roth

Kawaihae, Hawaii

DON'T JUDGE GARDENING on the west side of the big island of Hawaii by Mrs. Roth's beautiful garden. It is extremely difficult—perhaps more so than in any part of the United States except Alaska. There are two reasons for this:

First, the island is nothing but one vast and still growing mountain of lava—basalt. In areas—particularly arid areas—which were buried under this ugly, heavy black stuff fairly recently, there is almost no plant life. (Lichens and tree ferns are usually the first plants to appear after an eruption—if they have moisture.) In the area in which Mrs. Roth has her home, the volcanoes have been inactive long enough to give nature a chance to cover the lava with a thin layer of soil and coarse grass. But this was so very thin on Mrs. Roth's building site that it was necessary to use jackhammers and dynamite to make holes for every tree and large shrub, and then to bring in countless truckloads of soil to fill the holes and to build up sufficient soil depth for the lawn and smaller shrubs.

The second difficulty in gardening on the west side of Hawaii is in finding enough water. Rainfall at Kawaihae measures only eleven inches a year. (One of the state's rain forests is a few miles away in the mountains north of nearby Kamuela, but most of the streams originating there flow eastward except after storms.) Consequently it is necessary to draw heavily on the public water supply to keep anything alive. In fact, Mrs. Roth's sprinkler system and hoses are going almost every day from morning to night.

One other problem that gardeners on Hawaii (and Kauai) face is the fact that their island has fewer types of insect and fungous pests than the main island of Oahu. All plants shipped to Hawaii from Oahu must be specially disinfected. This makes it impossible to secure anything but small plants. As a result, Mrs. Roth had to depend for large specimens on whatever she could find on her home island (which because of its small population does not have many well-stocked nurseries).

But as I indicated earlier, Mrs. Roth's garden gives no hint of the existence of these problems.

The garden was started early in 1965. The site is one of the most beautiful imaginable. It is on a small promontory dominated by a great distorted lava rock. Immediately to the north beyond one of Mrs. Roth's small sandy beaches is a rocky point topped with a graceful, windblown specimen of the algaroba. To the south, looming in the

The sharp, jumbled black lava rocks that edge the shore are as much a part of the garden as the carefully planted palms and flowering shrubs and trees

Cool terrace outside living and dining room centers on huge rock at point of property. The plants in tubs help to reduce maintenance work in garden.

GARDEN OF MRS. WILLIAM P. ROTH   159

Planting in garden was limited to avoid competing with the setting and to simplify upkeep and because big planting holes must be dug with dynamite

Covered entrance walk is lined with tubbed plants. Open lawn on either side separates the four parts of house yet has effect of pulling them all together.

distance over the coconut palms that Mrs. Roth planted to screen out an adjacent resort hotel are 8,300-foot Hualalai, an extinct volcano, and 13,700-foot Mauna Loa, which last erupted in 1960. To the east, visible above the brown hills that roll down to the sea, is mighty Mauna Kea, another extinct volcano.

Because of the you-must-see-it-to-believe-it quality of this setting and because this is Mrs. Roth's vacation home and because she already owned one of the world's greatest gardens, everybody involved in the development of this garden worked toward one goal—simplicity: don't compete with the scene; don't do anything that requires a great deal of care. To this end, planting has been limited mainly to trees and shrubs—and there are not too many of these, considering the size of the garden. (On the ocean side there are exactly three trees, all sea grapes.) Immediately next to the house, many plants are in tubs.

Mrs. Roth has not, however, allowed easy maintenance to do her out of plenty of color. A small *arroyo* on the mountain side of the driveway and visible from many parts of the house is planted solidly with white hibiscus, cream-colored plumerias, bougainvillea of mixed colors and allamanda. And there are two jacaranda trees in the grassy courtyards between the wings of the house.

Lily pool is center of one of few areas that might be called landscaped. It is at edge of Mrs. Wichman's jungle garden. Anthuriums grow on the far side.

Garden of

Mrs. Juliet Wichman

Haena, Hawaii

G EOLOGICALLY SPEAKING, the islands of Hawaii were born yesterday. They consisted of molten lava, and since they were far removed from the rest of the world, the only way they acquired any plant life was by courtesy of winds, ocean currents, birds, and, only recently, men. Consequently, you might think that they have no native flora. But surprisingly, they do. Almost 95 per cent of the different plants growing in the islands today are not found elsewhere in the world. One of the main reasons for this is that the Hawaiian Islands are a paradise. Plants grow so much better there that new and better varieties are constantly developing.

The island of Kauai—the "Garden Island," oldest and northernmost of the islands—is particularly hospitable to plants. And nowhere is it more so than on the northern coast in the general vicinity of Haena. The soil is the same rich, coarse, reddish stuff found elsewhere on the island. The rocks are the same porous black lava rocks. The hours of daylight are the same—about twelve in winter and fourteen in summer. The temperature averages the same 75 to 78 degrees. But situated at the base of the mountains that are first struck by the trade winds, Haena has a total annual rainfall of between 70 and 100 inches—more than twice as much as falls on the county seat of Lihue, on the southeast coast only forty miles away. (Mrs. Wichman recalls one fantastic storm that dumped 42 inches of rain on Haena in just forty-eight hours. During the same period, Lihue was dry.)

It is mainly because of this heavy rainfall that Mrs. Wichman's garden is unusual. There are few if any places in the United States where a tropical jungle—which is what this garden is—grows right beside the sea. True, there is one other seaside garden on Kauai that has many of the same plants, but they owe their existence in large part to an extensive man-made watering system.

Mrs. Wichman bought the property in 1947. It had once had a good garden, but for years that had not been touched. When Mrs. Wichman arrived, she had to bring in a gang of men to chop away the dense growth. Then she started to rebuild virtually from scratch. More or less below the house, which is a vacation home, is a small lawn; then the narrow highway, little traveled; and then the beach, which would quickly grow up with trees if allowed. Above the lawn is a small swimming pool fed with spring water from the mountains. Then the jungle begins. It climbs up the lower slopes of the mountain towering directly above the house until it fetches up against a perpendicular cliff. Here in the deep shade mangoes crash every few minutes from the towering trees into the underbrush.

Mrs. Wichman is not a rare plant collector. She says her only interest has been in putting in tropical and semitropical plants that are easy to grow. But her garden contains many species. As you walk along the paths that wander through the two and one-half acre cultivated area you find that these are in large part grouped—ferns here, then gingers and heliconias, then bananas, then a small planting of anthuriums, then a few of the plants used by the early Hawaiians, etc. But inevitably, as in any jungle, there is considerable intermixture of plants. And in the darker areas the large-leafed philodendrons and monsteras are everywhere climbing over the trees like Jack's giant beanstalk.

To one who is not used to such plants, the garden seems incredible. But most of all it is exciting. Exciting in the sense that you feel that something dangerous might jump upon you from the unbelievably tight, lush, colorful growth—though you know perfectly well that such things don't happen in gentle Hawaii. Exciting, also, in the sense that it stimulates the senses. For here is the perfect interplay of beautiful plants in an idyllic setting.

Small front lawn opens up view of deserted white beach and blue sea. Coconuts collect beside wall. Philodendrons and monsteras climb everywhere.

Looming high behind the garden (and part of it) are fantastic peaks. They break the tradewinds and help to produce heavy rain on which jungle thrives.

In Mrs. Wichman's garden the foliage is almost as colorful as the flowers.
These are hybrid ti plants. Up the path a way are bananas equally brilliant.

*Because it is guarded by mountains on three sides, the Tanner garden enjoys
a slightly milder climate than gardens in Phoenix (behind camera to south)*

Garden of

Mr. and Mrs. L. A. Tanner

Phoenix, Arizona

I T TAKES A GARDENER four years to find out what goes on in this part
of the country," F. J. MacDonald, of the landscape architectural
firm of MacDonald and Bigler, says about the Phoenix area. He does
not mean to be taken literally, but there is no doubt that even for a
skilled and widely read gardener, a move to the desert country is
puzzling. Things just do not work out the way they are supposed to.

The soil is the first problem. It is devoid of humus. Not far beneath
the surface is a rock-hard layer of calcium salts—caleche—which
must be dug out for any large plant to establish a root system. Worst
of all, the pH content ranges from 7.4 to 8.1. Without the constant addition of iron chelates, most plants are affected by chlorosis.

Water is the second problem. Unlike other Southwestern towns,
Phoenix has plenty. But what gushes from the pipes has a pH of over 7.
Consequently, even though the soil alkalinity can be lowered by
digging in peat, sulfur, and gypsum, the water is constantly working
to raise it again. As a result, only plants that are genuinely alkali-
resistant thrive.

The sun, of all things, is the third problem. It is so intense that if
plants are not oriented precisely to their specifications, they will wither
away and die. In other words, taking a chance on planting a shade-
lover on anything but the north side of a building is fatal.

These problems were well known to Mr. MacDonald when he designed the Tanner garden a number of years ago. He therefore selected and placed his plants so carefully that they are still in excellent condition. The only garden casualty has been, not a plant, but a small water pump. Like most such pumps in the area, it was put out of commission by dust and calcium deposition.

Mr. and Mrs. Tanner's home is fortunately situated part way up a hill studded with tall cacti. It commands a sweeping view of the city a

Terrace around pool and extending under roof overhang is on same level as living room. For this reason, garden is an inseparable part of house interior.

Desert sunlight places a limitation on what can be grown in the open, but in the lee of the north wall of the Tanner house shade-loving plants do well

few miles to the south. And because it is guarded on the east, west, and north by mountains, it is protected from the winter winds and frosts. For this reason, it has its own micro-climate—the equivalent of Zone 9. (Phoenix proper is in Zone 8.)

In landscaping the place, Mr. MacDonald capitalized on both site and climate. In front of the house, where the land falls off to the street

A common practice in the desert is to make gardens copy nature. But Mr.
MacDonald chose to make the Tanner garden a foil for nature and vice versa.

and then slants upward to a high peak, he was able to persuade the excavating contractor to preserve some of the rock outcroppings that give the hills their rough-hewn character. These are handsome in their own right and also help to tie the property into the countryside and to atone for the unavoidable expanse of street and driveway. In back of

Excavating contractor was persuaded to preserve the raw outcroppings between street and house. The bank is planted with carissa and bougainvillea.

GARDEN OF MR. AND MRS. L. A. TANNER   173

In the heavy shade that blankets front entrance on north side of house, jungle plants grow with abandon. Counting these, garden has over 100 varieties.

the house, where Mr. MacDonald located the main garden area, he left the land pancake flat and on exactly the same level as the living and dining rooms, which open on to it. Thus, sitting indoors, you can at once enjoy the view of the garden—which here consists of a covered terrace area, swimming pool, and rather sparse planting—and the grand mountain vista beyond. Because the two sights are dissimilar— the near one being predominantly white and green and geometric; the far one being blue and gray and rugged—each complements and accents the beauty of the other. (By contrast, most gardens in the Tanners' neighborhood attempt—usually rather badly—to duplicate nature and consequently contribute nothing to the natural scene and gain nothing from it.)

The plant materials Mr. MacDonald used also contain contrasts, although many of these are apparent only after you have toured the entire garden several times. There are well over one hundred varieties (an extremely high figure for the desert country). They include the following:

Asparagus sprengeri
Bambusa falcata
Bougainvillea
Callistemon lanceolatus
Cape honeysuckle
Carissa grandiflora
Chamaerops excelsa
Cocculus laurifolius
Cycas revoluta
Dracaena draco
Euonymus japonicus
Ficus (various kinds)
Hedera canariensis
Ilex burfordii
Lantana camara
Liriope spicata
Loquat
Olive
Philodendron (various kinds)
Phoenix date palm
Pyracantha graberi
Ulmus parvifolia sempervirens
Viburnum suspensum
Wandering Jew
Washington palm

The small patch of lawn is made with a hybrid Bermuda grass.

Four photographs by Ezra Stoller

*White bridge leads from main part of house (unseen to right) across swim-
ming pool to a small "wild" pool bordered with rocks, flowers, and grasses*

Garden of

Mr. and Mrs. Clint Murchison, Sr.

Dallas, Texas

H ERE IS A FAIRYLAND GARDEN for swimming and for entertaining. It was created for Mr. and Mrs. Murchison by the Lambert Landscaping Company when a new wing—a combination bathhouse and entertainment center—was added to the house.

A more ingenious, more complex garden is hard to conceive of. But imagine the pleasure on a sunny afternoon of swimming lazily back and forth under the white bridge that crosses the pool; or the delight of dining on the slate terrace surrounded by trees, shrubs, and walls that are splashed with soft electric moonlight.

The garden is a crescent surrounded by a high brick wall and iron fence. In the center is the blue swimming pool, also crescent-shaped. Water enters the shallow end through a stylized channel with a bed of smooth, round, colorful river stones. The channel flows out from under a glass-walled gallery connecting the new wing to the main house. At the rear of the gallery and visible from it is the source of the water—a shallow pool bordered by small trees and flowers and walled around with brick. This is a Japanese garden in miniature, with a stone lantern, round stepping-stones across the pool and an idol seen through an iron gate at the far end.

Yet another small pool lies across the swimming pool at the end of the bridge leading from the house. It is strewn with rocks and bordered with flowers and grasses to resemble a woodland pool.

Planting in this intimate, enchanting water garden is limited by the climate and by the small scope of the garden (which is also partly attributable to the climate). Dallas averages less than 3 inches of rainfall a month. There are extreme hot spells and sudden bitter cold spells. The wind blows—sometimes fiercely. And to add to the gardener's difficulties, the soil is very heavy and alkaline.

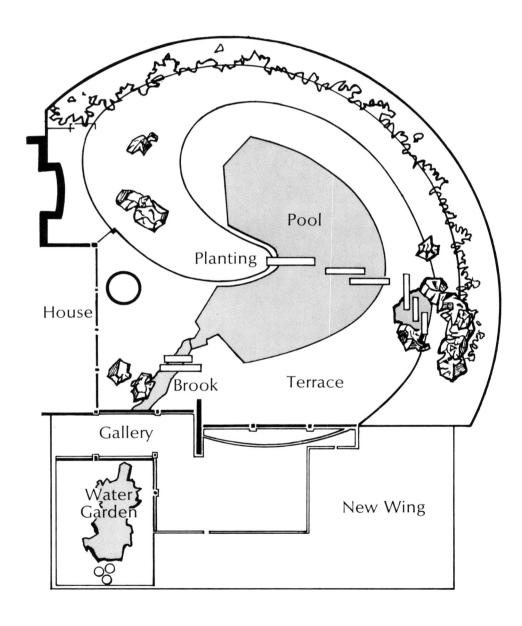

Water enters swimming pool through this stylized, stone-strewn channel. In courtyard behind glass-walled gallery is a miniature Japanese water garden.

Landscape architect J. O. Lambert feels that for all but the most avid gardeners the Dallas small-plant list is best limited to about twenty broadleaf evergreen shrubs and a dozen flowering plants. In the Murchisons' garden, he relied mainly on the following:

Ajuga reptans
Aucuba japonica
Azalea
Bamboo
Caladium
Camellia japonica (rather rare in Dallas)
English ivy
Liriope spicata
Live oak
Red oak
Tulip
Wisteria
Yaupon holly

Exotic Japanese garden is the source of water that enters crescent-shaped swimming pool. Like the main garden area, it is beautifully lighted at night.

Garden is a fairyland of blue, green, black, and white in the early spring.
Later, caladiums are the principal source of color. Plant list is limited.

In the Hardmans' circular garden, diamonds are the persistent theme, appearing in the metal gazebo, the gate, and the ivy trained on the white stone wall

Garden of

Dr. and Mrs. Thomas J. Hardman

Tulsa, Oklahoma

I N A CAGE in the back of Dr. and Mrs. Hardman's gazebo lives a pair of white fan-tail pigeons. They bespeak the delicate femininity of the garden that lies in a semicircle before them and that flows around the ends of the house to the front door.

Femininity is a rare quality in gardens, and I do not pretend to understand why. You can make a case for the fact that most landscape architects are men. On the other hand, consider how much of all gardening—especially creative gardening—is done by women. But no matter. A beautifully turned-out feminine garden is a joy and we could do with many more of them—especially more like this one.

It was designed for Mrs. Hardman in 1952 by J. O. Lambert, of the Lambert Landscape Company, Dallas. Mr. Lambert has a special flair for walled gardens, and here he was at his best. The wall sets the tone of the entire garden. It is a white-painted stone, and curves around the rear garden area in a big, slightly imperfect semicircle. Ivy trained on wires forms a light, open diamond pattern on the inner surface.

Inside the wall is a flower border; then a brick walk leading to the gazebo (which is made of painted metal and repeats the diamond pattern); then a wider border with tulips, ajuga, some small trees, and a neat, low holly-hedge edging; and then in the center of the concentric semicircles, the lawn.

The lawn at the center of the wheels-within-wheels garden basks in the warm sun a few steps down from the stone terrace across back of house (right)

One of the garden's most colorful areas is at the sunporch end of the house.
Here behind an unusual wood-strip fence is a mass of big, brilliant azaleas.

A flagstone terrace shaded by two spreading elms—one American and one Chinese—overlooks this joyous scene.

The garden in front and at the sun-porch end of the house is less feminine, less patterned. Here the yard is enclosed by an unusual fence made of unfinished wood strips strung together—but not quite touching—on iron pipes hung between square stone posts. Inside are more tulips, dogwoods, and fine azaleas. An old southern magnolia is espaliered on the two-story wall beside the front door.

Mrs. Hardman has pictures of the garden when it was fairly new. They indicate that it has changed hardly at all over the years. This is a tribute to its owner's patience and proud interest, for there are easier places to garden than Tulsa.

The soil is rather poor and underlaid with rock. To start the garden, Mrs. Hardman had to bring in lots of what her gardener calls "black dirt" and sand. This needs to be changed occasionally in the borders.

The climate, as in other Plains States, is harsh. Precipitation in Tulsa averages around 30 inches a year, which means that Mrs. Hardman's underground sprinkler system must be turned on about every three days during the growing season. The temperature has gone as high as 110 and as low as minus 3. Nevertheless, despite this frigid reading, the world begins to turn green in mid-March; but after that, sure as fate, there will be a frost. I visited Mrs. Hardman's garden on April 20, 1966, and gardeners I talked with throughout the city were complaining that their roses had been killed back twice by frosts. None predicted that it might not happen yet again.

In view of these conditions, it is not surprising that, although Tulsa and Long Island are both on the northern edge of Zone 7, many plants that thrive in the latter location do not do particularly well in the former. For instance, Mrs. Hardman's original dogwoods have already been largely replaced, whereas on Long Island at the same age they would be in their prime. Similarly, a number of Mrs. Hardman's azaleas have been replaced. On the other hand, who on Long Island has a *Magnolia grandiflora* that is 30 feet tall?

Such quirks of nature make gardening interesting. But it takes more than mere interest in gardening to create a garden as durably charming as this one.

Walk circling front lawn toward sunporch and main garden behind house is banked on left with tulips and azaleas. Dogwoods on right do not do well.

*In lieu of an abundance of color, Mrs. Zahm likes to emphasize the textures
of plants and materials, as in this grouping at the end of the swimming pool*

Garden of

Mr. and Mrs. George Zahm

Delray Beach, Florida

YOU COME to southern Florida expecting to be overwhelmed by the color of bougainvillea, hibiscus, and royal poinciana—and you are not disappointed: it is everywhere. Then, when you come upon this garden, there is something of a letdown. It is almost all green. True, there is some yellow and white bloom, and a very little red. But this garden—except for the blue of the swimming pool—is essentially green, green, green.

And much for that reason, you soon discover it is very pleasant. A place to relax. I was led to it by a friend who said, "It's so restful. From every room there's a lovely, quiet little vista. And the plants are beautiful."

The garden and house were built in 1961. They were planned as a unit. In addition to striving for an attractive, integrated scheme, Mrs. Zahm, who is a professional landscape architect and has done many gardens in Buffalo, where she and Mr. Zahm live half of the year, had several objectives: She wanted a garden with a great deal of texture. Texture, she feels, is as beautiful as color, longer lasting, and less distracting. She wanted an interesting, self-contained swimming pool area that would require the least possible maintenance. And she

To protect the fine Ormond Bermuda lawn from water splashed over the sea-wall by passing yachts, the Zahms put in this wide border of white gravel

wanted plants that would resist winds and salt air and that would bloom—if they bloomed at all—in winter and spring when she was in Florida.

Of course Mrs. Zahm attained these objectives. Credit belongs not only to her planning but also to the fact that she and Mr. Zahm have learned to cope with the problems of gardening in our southernmost mainland state:

1. The soil is so light and sandy that it is like a sieve. Water and fertilizer go right through it. At one time Mr. Zahm asked his gardener whether it would not be a good idea to work in peat moss. "You could put in a carload, Mr. Zahm," the man answered, "and the soil would just suck it away." The only type of humus that has any value is the muck dug out of the swamps. The Zahms applied a lot of this early in the game and continue to topdress with it occasionally.

Another drawback of the soil is its lack of natural nutrients. A balanced fertilizer—usually 6-6-6 or 8-8-8—must be applied twice a year. But even this treatment is sometimes inadequate. Then it becomes necessary to apply a prepared mixture of trace elements. Within a week or two, this will revive ailing plants and make them put on amazing growth.

2. Even though the average annual rainfall measures almost 60 inches, frequent watering is essential. Mr. Zahm is still adding to his already extensive sprinkling system.

3. Hurricanes are an annual threat, and there are also five-day "blows" when the wind is cold and never seems to stop. The hurricanes, of course, do extensive damage, but many trees that are toppled can be winched upright again (thanks to the lightness of the soil). The blows are less harmful, though plants frequently are left with a tattered look that lasts for some time.

4. Growth is lush, as a ride down any established residential street indicates. Most shrubs and vines grow in spurts two or three times a year. When they do, they need to be pruned hard; otherwise, they will eventually conceal the house they are supposed to ornament. One of the pleasantly unusual things about the Zahm garden is that the plants are in proper scale.

5. As in other parts of the country, good help is scarce. Many people parade as gardeners, but really know little about what they are doing. "And when you are away half of the year," Mr. Zahm says, "you want to know you have someone who is competent and reliable."

6. A good lawn requires a lot of attention. Most Floridians use St. Augustine grass or occasionally Bermuda grass, but rarely zoysia. Mr. and Mrs. Zahm elected for Ormond Bermuda, a new hybrid which has the look of golf-green Bent (Ormond is also used for greens). It must be kept very short and watered sparingly to prevent fungus diseases from setting in. Once a year, right after the Zahms leave for the North,

it is scalped close to the root tops and then cut vertically with rotating knives. "We consider this grass a luxury, but it's worth all the care it requires," Mr. Zahm says.

7. When the tide is high, the wash of yachts going up and down the Intracoastal Waterway sometimes goes over the sea walls. This wrecked the edges of the Zahms' lawn and also assisted the land crabs in undermining the soil behind the wall. To reduce the damage to the grass, the Zahms finally cut the lawn back about four feet from the wall and replaced it with white gravel. (The erosion continues.)

8. Few northern plants will survive the area's heat (Delray Beach is in Zone 10). Consequently, Mrs. Zahm's plant list, below, sounds familiar only to southern Californians, Hawaiians, and greenhouse gardeners. All species are evergreen.

> *Allamanda hendersonii*
> Calabash, black
> Calamondin
> *Carissa grandiflora* and hybrids
> *Clusia rosea*
> Coconut palm
> Coco plum
> *Comnocarpus erectus*
> Croton
> *Gardenia jasminoides*
> *Jasminum amplexicaule* and *simplicifolium*
> *Jatropha multifida*
> Juniper (*Juniperus chinensis pfitzeriana* and *conferta*)
> *Ligustrum japonicum*
> *Malpighia coccigera*
> *Mimusops balata*
> *Ochrosia elliptica*
> *Pittosporum tobira*
> *Podocarpus macrophylla*
> *Scaevola suaveolens*
> *Schefflera brassaia actinophylla*
> Sea grape
> *Stigmaphyllon lingulatum*
> *Thrinax*
> *Veitchia merrillii*
> *Viburnum odoratissima* and *suspensum*
> Yeddo hawthorn

Allamanda makes a bright spot on sunny terrace overlooking waterway. To protect area from falling coconuts, Zahms strip trees before nuts ripen.

A corner of Mr. Lannan's sculpture garden. Square bed of red petunias is a somewhat surprising but delightful note in such a modern, tropical setting.

Garden of

Mr. J. Patrick Lannan

Palm Beach, Florida

THIS GARDEN is an outdoor museum. It was established on an old property which slopes rather steeply (for Palm Beach) down from the oceanfront highway to Lake Worth. When Mr. Lannan purchased the place several years ago, the area behind the main body of the house was given over to a lawn running from the large living terrace to the lake. A narrower, parallel area behind the entrance court and garage was essentially jungle. While Frederic B. Stresau, Mr. Lannan's landscape architect from Fort Lauderdale, changed the lawn area to incorporate a swimming pool and a few big sculptures, he concentrated his efforts on the jungle area.

What he created—largely out of masonry—is a series of open rooms of classic design. You first enter a large square court which was formerly the turnaround area for the garage. You move into a long, wide "corridor" with three short flights of steps. This leads into the main museum area, consisting of a narrow walkway to a rose garden down the hill; an L-shaped terrace of native travertine, and a "jungle room" overhung by palms and banyan trees and with a large, dish-shaped reflecting pool in the center.

The modern sculptures, which are of various styles and sizes, are sparingly displayed throughout the entire garden. Several are given center-stage treatment; others look as if they were standing by, silently surveying the scene; still others you almost have to hunt for. (A small-ish stone piece set on the back edge of the reflecting pool is inconspicuous in the deep shadows.)

The planting in the garden is as prominent as the art works. It relieves the flat lines of the terraces, walls, and walks; casts shadows; adds color and texture. Hedges of *Viburnum sandankwa* grow in narrow planting pockets against some of the higher walls. Various espaliered trees are on three sides of the entrance court. A well-pruned sea grape gives partial protection against the sun to a clump of bromeliads. Red petunias crowd a plant pocket in the terrace floor. A graceful papyrus plant rises in the corner of a small square pool with the tiniest of fountains. Crotons brighten the shadowed reflecting pool area with their red and yellow and variegated leaves.

Other plants include the following: Trees—Hong Kong orchid, white orchid, yellow trumpet, mango, calamondin, grapefruit, key lime, fishtail palm, *Areca* palm, and *Clusia*. Shrubs—star jasmine, dwarf *Carissa*, coco plum, shell ginger, giant Japanese yew, *Crinum*, blue *Plumbago*, and oleander. Accent plants—bird of paradise, *Spathyphyllum*, Sumatran banana, and Australian tree ferns. Ground covers—*Liriope, Ophiopogon, Scindapsis*, wandering Jew, and *Wedelia*.

The rose garden, which is filled with color in April, is visible from about half of the sculpture garden, but the formality and masonry of the latter are missing from it. It seems, however, like a perfectly logical extension—and a very pleasant one—of the sculpture garden. The main reason for this is that the lathhouse and toolhouse, which look exactly alike although the former is open to the weather and the latter is not, have something of the feeling of several of Mr. Lannan's art works.

*Toolhouse at right is made of dark-painted plywood to protect tools and
covered with white wood strips to resemble lathhouse in which orchids grow*

Large green arrow dominates terrace at heart of sculpture garden. Terrace is raised slightly above reflecting pool (rear) and rest of surrounding area.

*Narrow walk makes a square around dish-shaped reflecting pool. Planting
of trees and shrubs, including colorful crotons, screens out lawn to left.*

In addition to sculpture garden, Mr. Lannan built pool behind main body of house. To left of chrome and yellow sculpture, lawn slopes down to waterway.

Looking from rose garden to sculpture garden's entrance. Immaculate area of white masonry and green plants was once jungle. Indoor gallery is at right.

Narrow paths and walks wind through the Costleys' wild garden, which is crammed with flowering shrubs and trees. Mr. Costley is a camellia fancier.

Garden of

Mr. and Mrs. Alton M. Costley

Atlanta, Georgia

IN THE BUCKHEAD SECTION of Atlanta, the mark of the well-tailored home is an expansive front lawn which sometimes constitutes almost the entire garden. Mr. and Mrs. Costley's home boasts not only an exceptionally fine lawn but—far more unusual—a large and delightful "wild" area in the rear. The two sections are completely dissimilar; but since the house and neatly screened parking area form a kind of neutral ground between them, and since both are distinguished by towering pines and bright azaleas, you move from one to the other without a jolt. On the contrary, the sharp contrast seems very pleasant.

The lawn speaks for itself; the wild garden (this is my name for it; the Costleys do not have one) has to be explored to be fully appreciated. It lies below the house on the side of a ravine that had to be partly filled in when Mr. and Mrs. Costley started work on the place in 1951. To provide a view down the hill from the house, the area is split from front to back by a long, narrow stretch of lawn. On either side of this and at the end are azaleas, rhododendrons, camellias, dogwoods, magnolias, crabapples, cherries, and larger native trees. They are planted close together and more or less at random. Narrow paths, which are paved in places where they might be washed out, meander in among them.

Pink brick terrace set into hillside is surrounded by white brick walls that
make an elegant background for handsome magnolia (in shadow) and espalier

The effect that the garden creates is of a wilderness with clear trails and without menace. You feel away from the racing world. Your pace slows. Around each bend in the path you expect to find some new horticultural delight.

An additional pleasant feature of the area is that it does not require a great deal of attention. As long as one plant does not crowd out another and as long as they do not obstruct the paths, they can be allowed to grow naturally. In the Southeast especially, this is an advantage.

As I drove around Atlanta with William C. Pauley, the Costleys' landscape architect, I could not help noticing how many handsome, more formal gardens have become overgrown. The reasons, Mr. Pauley said, are simple: (1) There is plenty of moisture and warmth to promote lush growth. (2) The clay soil is rich, and if it is well broken up and mixed with sand and peat, it further encourages growth. (3) The broadleaf evergreens to which most homeowners are addicted often give the appearance of looking larger than they are. (Like numerous landscape architects, Mr. Pauley deplores the popular Atlanta tendency to bypass the many good deciduous shrubs that will grow there.) (4) Good gardening help—especially men who understand the art of pruning—is scarce.

One other thing that you notice in touring Atlanta is that, despite the emphasis on lawns, they are obviously no easier to develop here than elsewhere. That Mr. and Mrs. Costley are unusually successful lawn-makers is simply attributable to the fact that they have found a formula that works and they are willing to stick to it no matter how great the effort and cost.

Their aim is to have a superb lawn from late September through June; a good one in July and August. To achieve this, they start in early September by having the grass cut as short as possible. Then the thatch is raked out by machine and the soil thoroughly aerated. Fertilizer is then applied and the lawn is seeded with a mixture of fescue and rye. This is watered in well (the Costleys have an underground sprinkling system). The rye comes up in ten days; the fescue in another seven. When the grass is three inches high, it is cut, and cut weekly thereafter. Fertilizer is applied at forty-five to sixty day intervals throughout the year, including winter.

Wild area, which was created in a partially filled ravine, is bisected by long, narrow stretch of lawn so that it can be more fully enjoyed from house

Lawn is beautiful all but one month of year. Tall pines with underplanting of azaleas are at one side. Grass does as well in the shade as in full sun.

The Banks's walled garden is resplendent with bloom from late March through October. It is but one of many colorful areas on the property.

Garden of

Mrs. William Nathaniel Banks

Newnan, Georgia

PUBLIC ASSUMPTIONS TO THE CONTRARY, very few private gardens in the Deep South are like the great public gardens for which the region is famous. But Mrs. Banks' is their equal. And it does not have the advantage of their age!

The late Mr. Banks began work on the garden when he built the house in 1929. In the succeeding years, the many plants that he, his wife, and his son set out, in accordance with the plan drawn up originally by landscape architect William C. Pauley of Atlanta, have made substantial growth; but there are not many cultivated specimens of the size found in some of the public gardens. Yet the garden bowls you over.

One reason for this is that there is about the over-all design a sense of what the younger Mr. Banks calls "inevitability." Many garden layouts seem purely arbitrary and therefore uncomfortable. But the entire garden here has logic and cohesion: as you walk from one area to the next, you anticipate what lies ahead; and although the beauty that you encounter may startle you, the garden element itself does not.

The central feature of the garden—or I might call it the cement that holds the whole thing together—is a great, wedge-shaped, shrubbery-bordered lawn which sweeps down from the house to a lake surrounded

Large, tree-rimmed lake that lies at the end of lawn behind house is unusual because, unlike other southern lakes, the water is not a murky, mud color

Peacocks and swans add to beauty of garden and also give it some of its old-time, formal air. Only other garden I saw with peacocks was the Websters'.

Mr. Banks believes that "water makes the greatest impression" in the garden.
Besides swimming pool and lake, there are several fountains and a lily pool.

on the far side by woods. The lake is a good illustration of the pains the family has taken to create the most beautiful possible surroundings. It is fed by a brook which in rainy weather used to carry quantities of silt. To keep this from muddying the lake water, Mr. Banks, Sr., built a settling pond and a channel to divert excess water around the lake. The result is a lake which, for the South, has unusual clarity.

To the right of the house, as you look out from it across the lake, are rhododendrons and azaleas bordering the driveway; a fountain in a paved circle surrounded by boxwood and dogwoods; and a future woodland garden with azaleas and camellias. There are still more azaleas and camellias bordering the woods across the driveway in front of the house.

The formal gardens are to the left of the house. Straight out from the living room is the lily-pool garden surrounded by boxwood and with borders crammed with tulips in spring and white periwinkle in summer. The garden is flanked by pink and white dogwoods and crimson azaleas. At right angles to this garden and visible from the lily pool is a rectangular swimming pool with a charming Venetian pavilion at the far end. Parallel with the swimming pool is a boxwood garden laid out in a maze pattern. From the end of this a path leads into a huge, formal, brick-walled flower garden.

Despite the splendid bloom that you find throughout the entire garden, the walled garden puts on a show that brooks no comparison. "We have flowers here from early spring until frost—roughly late March to late October," Mr. Banks reports. "There are five central beds with roses; five with peonies; three with chrysanthemums. These are bordered with narcissus. The borders which run all around the garden bloom as follows: In early spring, red and yellow tulips and blue Dutch iris bordered by yellow and blue violas. Then in later spring come foxglove, sweet William, and early daisies. This is when the peonies in the central beds are blooming and the roses are starting. The garden is at its height. In summer there are white phlox, blue stokesia, white lilies, yellow daylilies, marigolds, white and pink astilbe, white and pink zinnias, white and pink sultana, yellow cannas, plus some annual asters and cosmos with a blue ageratum border."

What was once scrubland is now a sculptured terrace of rounds and rings.
Only voices indicate presence of horsemen riding through pines below wall.

Garden of

Mrs. Audrey K. Kennedy

Southern Pines, North Carolina

WHEN MRS. KENNEDY BOUGHT this old estate for her winter home, the grounds were, in the words of Boston landscape architect Stanley Underhill, "sort of a jungle—nothing more than a tangled stand of long-leaf pine, honeysuckle, and catbrier." Today they are open, manicured, varied, and lovely.

The pines, which grow so luxuriantly in the acid red clay and sand of this part of the world (why else are Southern Pines and nearby Pinehurst so named?), still tower close by the big white house; but the underbrush has been cleared away so that the area's horsemen can ride through easily.

Directly in front of the house, in a triangle created by the main driveway, service road, and entrance court, is what amounts to a park —an expanse of lawn shadowed by handsome conifers, dogwoods, and a dense birch.

To the right of the entrance court, under the pines, is a splendid azalea garden. At the end of the grassy path through it stands a gazebo so graceful that even the surrounding flowers cannot compete with it.

At the lower end of the azalea garden, an iron gate leads to a very sculptured garden designed for Mrs. Kennedy's enjoyment when in her study or bedroom. It is partially enclosed by a white brick wall shaped like an open, well-turned letter J. Spotted around the enclosure with seeming casualness are three large, low, flat circles of clipped Japanese holly. The circle nearest the end of the garden is set off-center inside a lower ring of holly. Also in the ring and rising well above it is a stone Korean sculpture with a prominent vertical ring of its own.

Area directly behind the big house is a series of interconnecting yet visually separated terraces colored with dogwoods and shaded by the slender pines

Gate leads from the azalea garden to the terrace complex, which is divided by white walls. To the rear and well below, a meadow lies still under warm sun.

This garden connects in turn with two terraces across the back of the house. The upper terrace has two levels. The higher level is paved and edged with two small beds of azaleas. The lower level is in grass and has a small round pool with a gay figure of Pan sitting on a toadstool.

The main lower terrace, much enlarged from the way Mrs. Kennedy found it, is entirely in grass and edged with boxwood and other shrubs. Below it the land drops off sharply and opens out into a great, sunny meadow with a cloud of white dogwoods on the far side.

Bow window looks out on a paved, azalea-edged terrace and this grass terrace, which was lengthened at both ends when Mrs. Kennedy bought the estate

Mrs. Kennedy's garden was the first I visited when I started on this book. It was mid-April. The day was sunny and warm. The garden had a tranquillity which was almost soporific. At any rate, I did not realize until later how different the various sections of the garden are. The effect is rather like a house with a blue room, a green room, a red room, and so on. And yet the whole thing is held together by some mysterious thread. Just what this is I am still not sure but rather suspect it is simply the owner's and Mr. Underhill's ability to stamp what they create with an air of quiet elegance.

Delicate gazebo—one of Mr. Underhill's luckiest finds—stands on marble platform in azalea garden designed to satisfy Mrs. Kennedy's love of color

PLANT HARDINESS ZONE MAP

Agricultural Research Service
U. S. Department of Agriculture

Approximate range of
average annual minimum
temperatures for each zone

Zone 1 Below −50° F
Zone 2 −50° to −40°
Zone 3 −40° to −30°
Zone 4 −30° to −20°
Zone 5 −20° to −10°
Zone 6 −10° to 0°
Zone 7 0° to 10°
Zone 8 10° to 20°
Zone 9 20° to 30°
Zone 10 30° to 40°

The Hawaiian Islands are not
zoned. However, the average
annual minimum tempera-
ture at sea level is 70°

NFLD

N.S.

N.B.

ME

QUE

ONT

N.H.

VT

MASS

R.I.

CONN

BROOKLINE
BOSTON
GREENWICH
LARCHMONT
ISLIP
FLOURTOWN
CHESTNUT HILL
WASHINGTON

N.Y.

GREAT BARRINGTON

ROCHESTER

PA

MD

W. VA

VA

N.C.

S.C.

SOUTHERN PINES

GROSSE POINT SHORES

HIGHLAND PARK

MICH

OHIO

IND

KY

TENN

ATLANTA
NEWNAN

GA

ALA

MISS

LA

ARK

FLA

PALM BEACH
DELRAY BEACH

LAKE FOREST

ILL

ST. LOUIS

MO

IOWA

WIS

MINN

WAYZATA

MAN

N. DAK

S. DAK

NEBR

KANS

OKLA

TULSA

DALLAS

TEXAS

SASK

ALB

MONT

WYO

OGDEN

IDAHO

UTAH

NEV

COLO

N. MEX

ARIZ

PHOENIX

B.C.

WASH

ORE

CALIF

SEATTLE

SAN MATEO
HILLSBOROUGH
WOODSIDE
LOS ALTOS HILLS

LOS ANGELES
LAGUNA BEACH